Gift to

Sheila

From

Dirk

Message

A Daily Walk

Christian Art Gifts

A DAILY WALK by Selwyn Hughes

A compilation of excerpts from the original devotional booklets published under the title Every Day with Jesus by Selwyn Hughes.

© 1998: Christian Art,
P O Box 1599,
Vereeniging,
1930,
South Africa

Design by: Christian Art

ISBN 1-86852-404-3

Printed in Hong Kong.

JANUARY

In God's gymnasium

... train yourself to be godly.
1 Timothy 4:7

To be lean and fit spiritually should be the aim of every one of Christ's disciples. The biggest problem in the contemporary Church is that Christians regularly report unfit for duty. And a big part of their unfitness results from lack of spiritual exercise. How do we keep our physical bodies in trim? We do it by exercising. It is now a well known fact that to lose excess weight it is helpful to do more than dieting. Just as physical exercises increase the body's fitness and health, so spiritual exercises improve spiritual fitness and vitality. Godliness does not just happen. We have to train ourselves for it. There is no other way to find health for the soul.

For reading & meditation – 1 Timothy 4:7

Right acts – wrong motives

But by the grace of God I am ...
1 Corinthians 15:10

Christians are likely to fall into one of two errors concerning the matter of developing godliness. One is to depend on ecstatic spiritual experiences; the other is to depend on disciplined effort. Relying solely on either is wrong. Though ecstatic spiritual experiences are to be treasured, it is a mistake to use them as the basis for spiritual growth. Then to regard disciplined self-advancing effort as the secret of becoming a godly person is also an error. Paul was one of the most disciplined disciples in history, yet he gave the credit for his spiritual progress not to his disciplined living but to the grace of God: "by the grace of God I am what I am".

For reading & meditation – 1 Corinthians 15:1-11

Dependable disciples

... do not use your freedom to indulge the sinful nature ...
Galatians 5:13

Although the Christian message is that we draw our life and strength from God, nevertheless, in order to do that, we must be disciplined. Often "free grace" has been preached in such a way that it has weakened character. Paul warns against this in the passage before us today: "do not use your freedom to indulge the sinful nature". The effective Christian life is a balanced life. Being dependent means we draw our life from Another; being disciplined means we pay attention to the ways by which we draw from that Other. Dependence plus discipline makes dependable disciples.

For reading & meditation – Galatians 5:1-15

Discipline without direction

For those God foreknew he also predestined to be conformed to the likeness of his Son ...
Romans 8:29

When it comes to discipline in the Christian life many believers feel that practice is tiresome and tedious. God's great goal for us is to make us like Christ. In fact we are predestined for that – God's grace is working in our lives to make us like Christ. But if we are *predestined* to be conformed to Christ's image, what need is there of discipline? Because it is through discipline that we assent to God's purposes for our lives. Spiritual discipline puts us in a position where we will receive the grace that flows from the heart of our Saviour.

For reading & meditation – Romans 8:28-39

JANUARY 4

Love that "springs"

The goal of this command is love, which comes from a pure heart and a good conscience and a sincere faith.
1 Timothy 1:5

We don't usually connect discipline with spontaneity, but this is what the apostle Paul seems to be doing in this text. Discipline produces a love that "springs", he says. Society today has a false idea of freedom. Liberty comes from obedience to law. No law – no liberty. That is the way life works. Any supposed freedom that leaves you with an impure heart, a bad conscience, and an insincere faith ends not with a love that springs but with a love that sighs. And a love that sighs soon dies. A disciplined person has a love that springs – and a love that sings.

For reading & meditation – 1 Timothy 1:1-11

God's only published work

All Scripture is God-breathed and is useful for teaching, rebuking, correcting and training in righteousness ...
2 Timothy 3:16

Godly people are disciplined people. No spiritual exercise is more important than reading, studying and meditating on the Scriptures. The reason should be obvious. The Bible is God's one and only published work. Other books may draw their inspiration from the Scriptures, but the Bible is the only book that has upon it the stamp of divine infallibility. If we are to know God and train ourselves for godliness we must dip into the Word of God frequently. The number of committed Christians who spend time studying the Bible daily, or even regularly, is astonishingly low.

For reading & meditation – 2 Timothy 3:12-17

Hearing the Word of God

Until I come, devote yourself to the public reading of Scripture, to preaching and to teaching.
1 Timothy 4:14

A verse in Romans 10 says: "faith comes from hearing the message, and the message is heard through the word of Christ". Now that does not mean a person can come to faith in Christ only by *hearing* Scripture for, as history shows, multitudes have come to know the Lord through reading it for themselves. It is important for God's people to sing, praise and worship him but it is also important for them to hear his Word. We must exercise ourselves to listen to that Word. But how can we do that if, when we go to church or a meeting, the Bible is not read?

For reading & meditation – 1 Timothy 4:1-16

Reading the Bible

Man does not live on bread alone, but on every word that comes from the mouth of God.
Matthew 4:4

The daily or regular intake of the Scriptures is not only "the first exercise of the soul"; it is also the broadest. If you want to become more like Jesus and reflect his character then discipline yourself to read the Scriptures. "Surely we have to be realistic and honest with ourselves to know how regularly we need to turn to the Bible. How often do we face problems, temptations and pressures? *Every day!* How often do we need instruction, guidance and greater encouragement? *Every day!* How often do we need to hear God's voice, feel his touch, know his power? The answer to all these questions is the same: *every day!*"

For reading & meditation – Matthew 4:1-11

JANUARY 8

Every day with Jesus

Now the Bereans were of more noble character ... for they ... examined the Scriptures every day ...
Acts 17:11

Hearing and reading the Word of God are important and effective spiritual exercises. So also is studying it. The more you study the Bible the more you will grow. When the apostle Paul was languishing in prison and anticipating the arrival of his young friend Timothy he said: "When you come, bring the cloak ... especially the parchments" (2 Tim. 4:13). In cold and miserable conditions the apostle asked for two things: something for his body and something for his soul. Paul witnessed some wonderful events and had touched heaven, but he still wanted to delve into the Word of God until the day he died.

For reading & meditation – Acts 17:1-15

Read less – meditate more

My heart grew hot within me, and
as I meditated, the fire burned ...
Psalm 39:3

One of the tragedies of our day is that meditation is linked more to non-Christian systems of belief than it is with Biblical Christianity. The world has adapted the principle of meditation for its transcendental meditation and Biblical meditation. Meditation is deep focused thinking. Only about 1 per cent of Christians engage in this spiritual exercise. How sad. We read the Word, study it – both good spiritual exercises – but we will never get the best out of it until we know how to meditate on it. "The reason we come away so cold from reading the Word is because we do not warm ourselves at the fire of meditation."

For reading & meditation – Psalm 39:1-13

Regular respiration

Then Jesus told his disciples a parable to show them that they should always pray and not give up.
Luke 18:1

The second spiritual exercise is prayer. One of the major reasons for lack of godliness is prayerlessness. A tiger's first objective when it attacks another animal is to slit its throat with its sharp claws. When the animal is no longer able to breathe it is finished. Satan, the enemy of our souls, follows this same strategy in his attack on us. If he can stop us breathing spiritually by preventing us from praying, then we become powerless and a plaything in his hands. There can be no advance towards godliness unless you give time to prayer.

For reading & meditation – Luke 18:1-8

God's "VLE" (Very Large Ear)

Call to me and I will answer you and tell you great and unsearchable things you do not know.
Jeremiah 33:3

A writer commenting on the VLE (a large radio receiver in New Mexico) said: "God too has a VLE – a Very Large Ear."

Ethel Romig Fuller writes: *If radio's slim fingers can pluck a melody*
From night – and toss it over a continent or sea,
If songs like crimsoned roses are
culled from thin blue air,
Why should mortals wonder if God
hears and answers prayer?

For reading & meditation – Jeremiah 33:1-9

Christ expects us to pray

He said to them, "When you pray, say:
Father, hallowed be your name ..."
Luke 11:2

The Gospels reveal quite clearly that Jesus thought those who loved God would want to read his Word and pray. Several times he asked people questions that went right to the heart of their understanding of the Scriptures, beginning with the words: "Haven't you read ...?" Prayer is not optional. Whether or not we think prayer is a good idea is irrelevant – Christ expects us to pray. When we become Christians we bring our lives under the authority of Christ and submit to his commands. And one of his commands is that we should always pray (Luke 18:1).

For reading & meditation – Luke 11:1-13

Every prayer answered

Before they call I will answer; while they are still speaking I will hear ...
Isaiah 65:24

Many times prayer is answered in a way that we human beings cannot see or understand. God hears and answers *every* prayer. He does so by giving us what we asked for, by saying "No" because what we have requested is not good for us, by giving us something different, or by answering our prayer in a way that is beyond our comprehension. Yet another reason why we do not pray more is because of selfsufficiency. Prayer is made only when something happens that is far too big to handle. Jesus said: "Apart from me you can do nothing" (John 15:5).

For reading & meditation – Isaiah 65:17-25

An important secret

... in everything, by prayer and petition, with thanksgiving, present your requests to God.
Philippians 4:6

The secret is to begin your prayer time with meditation. As our Lord expects us to pray, and to pray often, are you prepared to look at your prayer life and make a fresh evaluation of it? Our Lord prayed much. Do you want to be like him? Then discipline yourself to be a person of prayer. One thing is sure: after hearing, reading and studying God's Word, prayer is the next most important spiritual exercise.

For reading & meditation – Philippians 4:1-9

"Worth-ship"

You are worthy, our Lord and God,
to receive glory and honour and power ...
Revelation 4:11

Worship most certainly is "the response of a heart in love with God", but how does the heart become filled with love for God? Though we do not develop love for God by self-effort we can focus the soul's attention on God, his attributes and character. The more we focus on God the more responsive we become to Him, and the more godly we become. Worship is ascribing proper worth to God, exalting Him and regarding Him as being deserving of adoration and honour. The soul knows nothing of worship unless it has a deep understanding of the Almighty's intrinsic worth.

For reading & meditation – Revelation 4:1-11

In awe of God

My ears had heard of you but now my eyes have seen you.
Job 42:5

Worship begins with a focus on God and a consideration of his worth. And the more we understand how worthy he is the more our souls are filled with awe. Most believers know how to pray and praise, but how often do we stand in awe before God? Job developed a sense of awe as a result of God's dealings with him. Daniel responded in a similar way. After God had addressed him he said: "I stood up trembling" (Dan. 10:11). We will never be able to truly convey to others what God means to us unless we know what it is to stand in awe before him and tremble at his glory.

For reading & meditation – Job 42:1-6

Worship – God's right

For great is the Lord and most worthy of praise; he is to be feared above all gods.
1 Chronicles 16:25

Worship is focusing on the greatness, the glory and the supreme worth of God and responding to him in adoration and awe. All right-minded people respond to beauty in exactly the same way – with admiration and awe. Just as a glorious sunset evokes a spontaneous response, so the soul cannot encounter the worthiness of God without responding in true worship. If, at this moment, you could catch a glimpse of how worthy God is, how beautiful his character, how glorious his nature, the inevitable consequence would be that you would fall on your face and worship him.

For reading & meditation – 1 Chronicles 16:7-36

"In spirit and in truth"

For it is we who ... worship by the Spirit of God ...
Philippians 3:3

God reveals himself to us in many different ways. Creation is just one of them. God has made himself known to us also through the Person of his Son, the Lord Jesus Christ. He came to this earth, lived and died, rose again, and ascended to the Father. Another way in which God reveals himself to us is through his Word, the Bible. How do we worship "in spirit and in truth"? We do so when we have the Spirit of God within us and live our lives according to the truth contained in the Scriptures. That is why meditation on God's Word is an essential prerequisite not only for prayer but also for worship. Worship reaches its highest point when God is being contemplated.

For reading & meditation – Philippians 3:1-11

Praise and worship

Within your temple, O God,
we meditate on your unfailing love.
Psalm 48:9

Prayer involves talking to God and God talking to you. Praise is thanking God for the things he has done, is doing, and is going to do. Worship is adoring God not so much for what he does but for who he is. Some Christians think of worship as something they do only on Sundays when they meet with other Christians in church. "If you will not worship God seven days a week you do not worship him on one day a week." We cannot expect to enter into worship on the Lord's Day if worship has not flowed from our hearts over the preceding six days. Corporate worship must never be a substitute for individual worship.

For reading & meditation – Psalm 48:1-14

"Open-doored to God"

At daybreak Jesus went out to a solitary place.
Luke 4:42

James Russell Lowell says of solitude:

If the chosen soul could never be alone
In deep mid-silence, open-doored to God,
No greatness ever had been dreamed or done;
The nurse of full-grown souls is solitude.

What does seeking solitude entail? It involves temporarily withdrawing from activity and finding a quiet or private place in order to rest, relax and give oneself to spiritual purposes. Our Lord often sought solitude. Involvement with people and ministry to others is important, but so also is solitude. The art is to know which of these is the priority of the moment.

For reading & meditation – Luke 4:38-44

JANUARY 21

"Islands of solitude"

Be silent before the Sovereign Lord,
for the day of the Lord is near.
Zephaniah 1:7

A large section of the population today, especially the young, seem afraid of being alone. Those who do not have what someone has called "islands of solitude" soon become frantic personalities. Kenneth Fearing says:

And wow they died as wow they lived,
Going zoom to the office, and whoosh home to sleep.

Jesus found solitude essential. It may be helpful to find a tranquil spot away from noise and other people. But much more is required. We need to be silent before our God.

For reading & meditation – Zephaniah 1:1-13

"Not enough silence"

And after the fire came a gentle whisper.
1 Kings 19:12

"A day is an ideal time but even half a day can bring rich spiritual rewards. Solitude can be found in a quiet place at home, but wherever possible it is best to get away from home. A different environment can have a dynamic effect on the soul." What is the real point of exercising the soul through solitude? The primary purpose is to hear the voice of God more clearly and to equip ourselves to be of better service to others. Sometimes we need a time of solitude in order to hear more clearly what God is saying. T.S. Elliot put it thus: "Where shall the world be found, where will the word resound? Not here, there is not enough silence."

For reading & meditation – 1 Kings 19:9-18

Deepened understanding

... (Jesus) said to them, "Sit here while I go over there and pray."
Matthew 26:36

If we want to be like Jesus we must get away from people so that we will have more to offer when we are with others. Solitude deepens our understanding of people, increases our compassion for them, gives us a new freedom from our own concerns and heightens our sensitivity towards them. We are better able to give ourselves to others after giving ourselves to God during times of solitude. If you are saying to yourself now, "This makes sense but I'm too busy", then I would reply that the busier you are the greater your need of solitude.

For reading & meditation – Matthew 26:36-46

Settling down in God

... no hammer, chisel or any other iron tool was heard at the temple site while it was being built.
1 Kings 6:7

We as temples of the Holy Spirit need to be built up through times of quietness. The disciplined person is the person who does what needs to be done, when it needs to be done. All the great men and women of God have been disciplined people. And their discipline included finding time for solitude. The purpose of finding solitude is to train the soul for godliness, not to enjoy a break from normal duties. "Nothing great was ever done by anyone, in science, literature, or religion, who did not enjoy and know how to use solitude."

For reading & meditation – 1 Kings 6:1-13

Stewardship

Be very careful, then, how you live ...
making the most of every opportunity ...
Ephesians 5:15-16

An important spiritual exercise in which all Christians should participate is that of *stewardship*. The dictionary defines a steward as "a person who is entrusted with the possessions or interests of another". Stewardship can be seen in terms of three things: time, treasure and talents. No one can have a soul that is fit and healthy unless it is being exercised in the proper deployment of all three. Take the first – *time*. Certain marginal matters (not family duties and responsibilities) have to be deliberately neglected in order to focus on the task in hand. Sometimes the good has to be sacrificed on the altar of the best.

For reading & meditation – Ephesians 5:1-17

The test of time

Teach us to number our days aright,
that we may gain a heart of wisdom.
Psalm 90:12

Until we know the difference between the urgent and the important we will never become good stewards of our time. Our lives are often ruled by the urgent because we have never taken the time to put things in their proper order of priority. The man who influenced the world most – our Lord Jesus Christ – was a man with a leisured heart. He was never hurried, never flurried and never worried. Jesus always had time for the things that mattered. Don't let life push you; you will stumble if you do.

For reading & meditation – Psalm 90:1-17

God owns – we owe

The earth is the Lord's and everything in it.
1 Corinthians 10:26

"You can't be a follower of Christ unless he has access to everything you have, including your money." The use of our time is a mark of our spiritual maturity. The same is true of the way we use our money. The first thing we must do is to establish in our minds the fact that God is the owner of everything; we are owers. This means we are managers, or stewards, of what God has given us. The house or apartment you live in is God's property. The car you drive, the clothes you wear, the food you eat – all belong to God. Viewing life in this way can change your entire perspective.

For reading & meditation – 1 Corinthians 10:23-33

Steps to stewardship

If anyone asks you, "Why are you doing this?" tell him, "The Lord needs it ..."
Mark 11:3

You own nothing. Everything you have is a trust. You must give an account of everything you possess to God. This puts God in his rightful place and you in yours. You are not free to manage your material possessions as you like, but as *he* likes. Limit your spending to needs, not luxuries disguised as needs. Necessities contribute to life; luxuries choke. Make your will under God's guidance. You have a responsibility to leave something to your family, but consider also leaving something as an investment to be used for the kingdom's purposes.

For reading & meditation – Mark 11:1-11

Saved to serve

But I am among you as one who serves.
Luke 22:27

In the Bible God's people are referred to not only as his children but as his *servants* also. Recall how Paul starts his letters to the Romans, the Philippians, and his friend Titus: "Paul, a *servant* ..." Every Christian is a servant of God and, as the term suggests, servants *work*. Paul describes his service to God in Colossians 1:29 in these words: "To this end I labour, struggling with all his (God's) energy, which so powerfully works in me." We are saved to serve – and if we are not serving then quite simply we are not in training to be godly. God asks for our time, our treasure and our talents to be put to *his* use.

For reading & meditation – Luke 22:7-38

"You've gotta serve"

... he poured water into a basin and began to wash his disciples' feet ...
John 13:5

Whatever our talents, they have been given to us not simply for us to enjoy them but so we can serve others. "Not every act that *may* be done as a discipline *needs* to be done as a discipline. I will often be able to serve another simply as an act of love ... without regard to how it may enhance my abilities to follow Christ. There certainly is nothing wrong with that and it may, incidentally, strengthen me spiritually as well. But I may also serve another to train myself away from arrogance, possessiveness, envy, resentment or covetousness. In that case my service is undertaken as a discipline for the spiritual life."

For reading & meditation – John 13:1-17

FEBRUARY

Inflow – outflow

Jesus ... said, "Go home to your family and tell them how much the Lord has done for you ..."
Mark 5:19

To describe sharing as a discipline may sound strange to some, but such are the vagaries of human nature that if we do not discipline ourselves to do so we may never do so at all. We should discipline ourselves to share by deed and word what we have found as we have prayed and read the Word. Many fail to do this. They are earnest and regular in the way they take in, but not as disciplined in the way they give out. Training the soul to be godly requires that we discipline ourselves to share Christ with others – when appropriate – even though we may not be in an evangelistic frame of mind.

For reading & meditation – Mark 5:1-20

Ready and alert

Always be prepared to give an answer to everyone ... for the hope that you have ...
1 Peter 3:15

Seven out of ten Christians who share their faith with others come away feeling they have failed. The fear of failure is one of the chief reasons why people fail to share their faith. And when we fear something we avoid it. Instead we put our energy into the disciplines where we are more likely to notice results – prayer, reading the Bible, seeking solitude, and so on. Unless we have a disciplined approach to sharing our faith with others it simply will not get done.

For reading & meditation – 1 Peter 3:8-22

Witness for the defence

... and you will be my witnesses in Jerusalem, and in all Judea and Samaria, and to the ends of the earth.
Acts 1:8

What does being a witness involve? It means that Jesus is on trial again before the world, and every one of his disciples is called on as a defence witness. If we are silent we join the prosecution for he said: "He who is not with me is against me." We let him down and badly. And in the process we let ourselves down. A verse in Revelation says: "They overcame ... by the blood of the Lamb and by the word of their testimony." If the word of our testimony is silent then the blood of the Lamb is silenced and does not speak on our behalf.

For reading & meditation – Acts 1:1-11

Receptivity and response

Land that drinks in the rain ... and that produces a crop ... receives the blessing of God ...
Hebrews 6:7

Two matters constitute the heartbeats of the gospel: intake and outflow, receptivity and response. Here are the two actions so vital to Christian living – taking and giving. Land which absorbs the rain then produces a crop useful to those for whom it is farmed. This type of land receives a blessing from God. But if it only received and never gave – what would happen to it? Then it would be cursed. In 2 Corinthians we read the words: "he who supplies seed to the sower" (9:10). What would happen if the sower didn't use the seed? Most likely he would not get any more.

For reading & meditation – Hebrews 6:1-12

"Say so"

Let the redeemed of the Lord say this – those he redeemed from the hand of the foe ...
Psalm 107:2

Once we become Christians we have an impulse to share Christ with other people. In the first chapter of John there are three finds: Andrew finds Peter, Jesus finds Philip and Philip finds Nathaniel. The gospel is a gospel of finding, not keeping. Most of the people whose healing is recorded in the Gospels were brought to Jesus by another person. "I do all this for the sake of the gospel," said Paul, "that I may share its blessings" (1 Cor. 9:23).

For reading & meditation – Psalm 107:1-16

"In simplicity sublime"

Jesus replied, "Foxes have holes ... but the Son of Man has nowhere to lay his head."
Matthew 8:20

No one has ever demonstrated the sublimity of simplicity as did Jesus. His entrance into this world was simple. He was born in a humble cattle shed. He spent his life in a little village called Nazareth not as a king (which he was) but as a carpenter. When he started to preach his words were direct and straightforward. His way of life, too, was simple and uncomplicated. "Beauty," it has been said, "is an absence of superfluities." If that is so then none has been more beautiful than our Lord Jesus Christ. We must discipline ourselves to be like Jesus and be "rich in common sense; in simplicity sublime."

For reading & meditation – Matthew 8:14-27

"It's all too simple"

... unless you change and become like little children, you will never enter the kingdom of heaven.
Matthew 18:3

"The Christian life is the way of complete simplicity." The writer of Ecclesiastes had this to say: "God made man simple; man's complex problems are of his own devising" (7:29, Jerusalem Bible). One great difference between the Christian faith and every other religion is its simplicity. To find God, says Scripture, you have to move away from all that is complicated to what is simple. Some people stumble over this very simplicity and reject the Christian message. A man I tried to lead to Christ, a doctor of philosophy, said, "It's all too simple." How sad.

For reading & meditation – Matthew 18:1-9

"Ouch, stop squeezing!"

Do not conform any longer to the pattern of this world, but be transformed by the renewing of your mind ...
Romans 12:2

"Don't let the world around you squeeze you into its own mould, but let God re-mould your minds from within, so that you may prove in practice that the plan of God for you is good, meets all his demands and moves towards the goal of true maturity." Today's heroes are people who go from poor to rich rather than those who give up their riches to become voluntarily poor. Until we understand the thinking of our sick society we will not be able to see how we are being squeezed into the world's mould – how much of the spirit of mammon we have absorbed.

For reading & meditation – Romans 12:1-8

Steps to simplicity

But seek first his kingdom and his righteousness, and all these things will be given to you as well.
Matthew 6:33

Seek first the interests of the kingdom. Let nothing come before your concern for the kingdom of God, including the desire for greater simplicity. Examine your life to see if complicated motives are producing anomalies in your attitudes and acts. Are you a person with mixed motives? Then that produces complications. Are you at war with yourself? Purify your motives inside and your conduct too will be right. Resist all attempts to persuade you to buy things for their status rather than their usefulness. Beware of feelings that override your common sense.

For reading & meditation – Matthew 6:25-33

FEBRUARY 9

"De-accumulate"

But I have stilled and quietened my soul,
like a weaned child with its mother ...
Psalm 131:2

Be alert to the possibility of becoming addicted to things. You must be a slave only to Christ. Cultivate a way of thinking that says not "What can I keep for myself?" but "What can I give away?" Refuse to be taken in by slick advertising. Cut out all affectation in speech and act. Go over your life and decide that everything you do and say will be true. Abandon such ploys as talking for effect and using weasel words. Live honestly before everyone. Then you will be able to say: "I have stilled and quietened my soul; like a weaned child" – weaned it from all that is complicated. Sublime.

For reading & meditation – Psalm 131:1-3

Fallacies about fasting

When you fast, do not look sombre as the hypocrites do ...
Matthew 6:16

To say that fasting can draw us back to legalism is to misunderstand Scripture. Fasting is also viewed with suspicion because we are influenced by the propaganda of our consumer society which encourages us to satisfy every appetite every day of our lives. A further reason is that the subject is not proclaimed from modern-day pulpits. To overlook fasting and ignore its Biblical significance is to deprive ourselves of an exercise of the soul that was taught and practised by our Lord, taken up by his disciples, and has been part of the life of the Church throughout its 2000 years of history.

For reading & meditation – Matthew 6:16-24

A cutting question

How can the guests of the bridegroom mourn while he is with them?
Matthew 9:15

Jesus responds by pointing out that guests at a wedding do not mourn or abstain from food during the festivities. Jesus said: "The kingdom of heaven is like a wedding feast and I am here to introduce it. My disciples are filled with joy, therefore it would not be appropriate while the Bridegroom is present for them to fast." Our Lord was giving here not only an intimation of his death but also of his Messiahship. However he added: "When the bridegroom will be taken from them; then they will fast" (v.15). Well, the Bridegroom *has* been taken away. But how many of his disciples fast?

For reading & meditation – Matthew 9:9-17

A futile fast

While they were worshipping the Lord and fasting, the Holy Spirit said ...
Acts 13:2

Sometimes it is helpful to consider what a thing is not before one can see what it is. People often abstain from food or cut down on their food intake to improve their health or lose weight. Fasting is not going without food in order to manipulate others. The fasting spoken of in Scripture is always for a spiritual, not a political or selfish purpose. Without the intention of discovering God in a greater way fasting can be a miserable experience. Although fasting is an important spiritual exercise, the motivation is of crucial importance.

For reading & meditation – Acts 13:1-12

The purpose of fasting

There ... I proclaimed a fast, so that we might humble ourselves before our God and ask him for a safe journey ...
Ezra 8:21

Many reasons for fasting are given in Scripture. One is to add power to our prayer lives. "Whenever men are to pray to God concerning any great matter, it would be expedient to appoint fasting along with prayer." A second reason is to discover God's guidance. Fasting does not guarantee that guidance will certainly be given but it certainly makes us more receptive to the One who guides. A third reason is to deepen the expression of an act of repentance. Joel 2:12 is just one verse that records God urging his people to show their sincerity by fasting.

For reading & meditation – Ezra 8:15-23

A day for decisions

Today, if you hear his voice,
do not harden your hearts ...
Hebrews 3:15

Biblical fasting must always have a spiritual purpose. There can be little doubt that God rewards fasting undertaken for a spiritual reason with great blessing. "Fasting," says one writer, "hoists the sails of the soul in hopes of experiencing the gracious wind of God's Spirit. It adds a unique dimension to one's spiritual life and helps the soul grow more Christlike." Fasting is commanded by God and is clearly taught in Scripture. Pray and ask God to guide you. All you need to say is: "Lord, I recognise this truth and I am willing to follow your leading." God will guide you as to the right times, the appropriate times.

For reading & meditation – Hebrews 3:1-15

FEBRUARY 15

"Good for the soul"

Then I acknowledged my sin to you
and did not cover up my iniquity ...
Psalm 32:5

Confession is owning up to God and others about the wrongs we have done, and *forgiveness* is being willing to wipe the slate clean regarding any who have wronged us. To find oneself in the wrong and do nothing about it is to condemn the self to live with a self one cannot respect. Repression is just as bad. When we drive guilt into the subconscious and shut the door on it we do not get rid of it. When sin is identified, exposed to the light of Christ and resolved through confession, joy returns to the soul. There is simply no other way out. All other routes lead to an incipient hell.

For reading & meditation – Psalm 32:1-11

To whom do we confess?

Cleanse me with hyssop, and I shall be clean; wash me, and I shall be whiter than snow.
Psalm 51:7

The awful thing about sin is not only that it breaks God's law but that it breaks his heart. We must tell him we are sorry about that, naming the transgression so that we are clear about what we are confessing. Have no fear as to how to approach God for access to God has been made easy through Jesus. If we have wronged others we must make confession to them too. Confession must always be as wide as the circle of offence. Confession must be wholehearted, without anything held back. Just one matter held back spoils it all – and cancels the rest.

For reading & meditation – Psalm 51:1-19

"I can't forgive"

But if you do not forgive men their sins,
your Father will not forgive your sins.
Matthew 6:15

If you do not forgive men their sins, your Father will not forgive your sins. By refusing others forgiveness you are breaking down the bridge over which you yourself must pass, namely that of forgiveness. Since God forgives you, you can forgive others. But if you exclude others from your forgiveness then you shut yourself off from God's forgiveness. Oh, the wonder of God's forgiveness. When we see how much we have been forgiven that in itself should be enough to send us out filled with joy to forgive others.

For reading & meditation – Matthew 6:1-15

"What's eating you?"

... forgive whatever grievances you may have against one another. Forgive as the Lord forgave you.
Colossians 3:13

There was a time when it was thought that an unforgiving person was just someone with whom it was difficult to get along – nothing more than that. Now we know the fallacy of that belief. The soul was not designed to harbour resentments, and when we force it to do so it rebels. Nothing can be more important to the soul's health than making sure the exercise of forgiveness is carried out regularly. Flush all bitterness out of your soul as you would flush a toxic substance out of your body. Say to yourself today: "My soul is too great to be the enemy of anyone."

For reading and meditation – Colossians 3:1-17

The way of the Master

Be kind and compassionate ... forgiving each other, just as in Christ God forgave you.
Ephesians 4:32

An unforgiving spirit is as harmful to the soul as poison is to the body so it follows that one of the most helpful exercises is to rid it of every trace of rancour. When we refuse to forgive we bring pain to the heart of our Lord. When nailed to a cross the Master prayed: "Father, forgive them, for they do not know what they are doing" (Luke 23:34). What greater joy can there be than having a soul free of guilt? Confession and forgiveness are the way to achieve that. But there must be no half-confessions, no partial forgiveness. Both must be full and frank and free.

For reading & meditation – Ephesians 4:17-32

Keep on keeping on

... let us run with perseverance the race marked out for us.
Hebrews 12:1

Perseverance – the dictionary defines the word as "the steadfast pursuit of an aim; constant persistence". So often we take up good things but don't carry them through. Our lives are strewn with the wreckage of good beginnings which became poor endings. In 1 Corinthians 16:9 Paul says: "I will stay on at Ephesus ... a great door for effective work has opened to me ... (but) there are many who oppose me." Our reaction might have been: "I am quitting. A great door for effective work has opened but there are too many who oppose me." It's not how you start but how you finish.

For reading & meditation – Hebrews 12:1-17

The Helper

So be careful to do what the Lord
your God has commanded you ...
Deuteronomy 5:32

Some people might say: "I'm the spontaneous type who finds it difficult to develop disciplined habits." If you are a Christian then the Holy Spirit dwells within you to make you like Christ. You may not be a disciplined or persistent person, but the Holy Spirit is. The Holy Spirit's task is to produce within you the desire and power to train yourself to be godly. Your task is to co-operate with the Spirit. As you yield yourself to him your natural temperament will come under his control. He will help you persevere. All you have to do is to provide the willingness.

For reading & meditation – Deuteronomy 5:22-33

Last but not least

But the fruit of the Spirit is love, joy, peace ... gentleness and self-control.
Galatians 5:22-23

Self-control is a fruit of the Spirit. It comes last on Paul's list, though that does not mean it is least in importance. Many systems, ancient and modern, would put self-control first. Confucius thought that self-control is what produces the "superior person". Hinduism teaches that breath- and thought-control will produce the "realised person". Stoicism, through will-control, tries to produce the "imperturbable person". The Christian message is that the Holy Spirit's direction produces a self-controlled person. We begin with love – love for Christ and love for others – and end up with self-control.

For reading & meditation – Galatians 5:16-26

Together

The one who calls you is faithful ...
1 Thessalonians 5:24

Self-control is a direct result of the Holy Spirit's control over a believer's life. When Christians express self-control by practising spiritual disciplines they find themselves growing in godliness. "God so cares for us that he himself helps us pray. The Holy Spirit prompts us and produces in us the desire to persevere in things." God is faithful in keeping us. Oh, how grateful we should be for this. He will always be faithful to his children and will help them persevere to the end. Our task is to yield ourselves to him, to make sure that our hearts are not hardened and that we stay alert and responsive to his promptings.

For reading & meditation –
1 Thessalonians 5:12-28

The Christian struggle

For physical training is of some value,
but godliness has value for all things ...
1 Timothy 4:8

"I thought the Christian life would be a bed of roses. I never realised it would be such a struggle." Such thinking results from wrong teaching – teaching that raises false hopes in people. Storms and high seas are as much the lot of Christians as they are of non-Christians. All Christians struggle from time to time – but we have the help of God in those struggles. Progress in Christian growth is made through a combination of God's effort and our effort. Those who teach "Let go and let God" are giving only half the truth. The other half is "we labour and strive".

For reading & meditation – 1 Timothy 4:1-16

Practice makes perfect

Whoever loves discipline loves knowledge ...
Proverbs 12:1

The path that leads to godliness is the practice of spiritual disciplines. Some people always look for short cuts and simpler ways of doing things and, while that may be acceptable as regards some aspects of living, it is not so in relation to the care of the souls. Is your spiritual life sporadic and spontaneous rather than directed? Most certainly we should not deride spontaneity, but spontaneity without discipline won't get us very far. Some people impress others with their spontaneity but deep down they lack discipline.

For reading & meditation – Proverbs 12:1-15

In training for eternity

... according to his eternal purpose which he accomplished in Christ Jesus our Lord.
Ephesians 3:11

Just as the spokes of a wheel hang loose without a hub so do the powers of life unless they are fastened to the central hub – the Lord Jesus Christ. He and he alone gives total meaning to life. This is why we must keep God and eternity in view while practising spiritual disciplines. The great revivalist Jonathan Edwards used to pray: "Oh God, stamp eternity on my eyeballs." Imagine the difference it would make if we saw everything from the viewpoint of God and eternity. To view discipline as simply relating to time is short-sighted. We are in training for eternity.

For reading & meditation – Ephesians 3:1-13

Great gain

But godliness with contentment is great gain.
1 Timothy 6:6

The central issue to keep in mind is this: development of the soul does not just happen. The soul has to be *trained* to be godly. Richard Foster, in his book *Celebration of Discipline*, said: "Superficiality is the curse of our age. The desperate need today is not for a greater number of intelligent people, but deep people." The way to God, we know, is through Christ, and the way to godliness is through the spiritual disciplines. Are you willing to commit yourself to ongoing training for godliness? Does being godly mean as much to you as getting a gold medal means to an Olympic contestant? "The alternative to discipline is disaster."

For reading & meditation – 1 Timothy 6:1-10

Fought and won

I have fought the good fight I
have finished the race ...
2 Timothy 4:7

Lord, what have I gained
if I eat wisely and well
but neglect to dine at your table;
if I work out faithfully
while failing to exercise love;
if I give myself to the pursuit of fitness
yet am not fit for your Kingdom?
Earthly disciplines fortify the body for a lifetime
Heavenly disciplines strengthen
the soul for an eternity.
Susan Lenzkes

For reading & meditation – 2 Timothy 4:1-7

MARCH

One faith, one Lord

... contend for the faith that was once for all entrusted to the saints.
Jude 1:3

We must not fall into the trap of thinking that Christianity is just one religion among many. Decidedly, it is not. Christianity is not just one religion among others; it is in a category all by itself. Some people say that one religion is as good as another. It sounds broad-minded but actually it is the judgment of ignorance. No one would ever make that statement if they understood the purpose of Christ's coming to this world, his atoning death on the cross, and his glorious resurrection. Jesus alone is the Light of the world, and thus utterly indispensable to salvation.

For reading & meditation – Jude vv. 1-16

No other Name

Salvation is found in no-one else, for there is no other name under heaven given to men by which we must be saved.
Acts 4:12

People seem to have given up the idea of syncretism mooted a couple of decades ago – the idea that all religions can be fused into one – and are focusing more on pluralism – the recognition of each faith as being of equal value. "It is high time that Christians should rediscover that Jesus Christ did not come to make a contribution to the religious storehouse of mankind, but that in him God reconciled the world unto himself."

For reading & meditation – Acts 4:1-12

Pluralism's persuasiveness

The life I live in the body, I live
by faith in the Son of God ...
Galatians 2:20

Christianity is unique, absolute, definitive, ultimate and final. Critics of the uniqueness of Christianity can be very persuasive. "The world is under great threat," they tell us, "because of environmental pollution, economic injustice, and many other problems. Nothing that divides us, including our religions, should be considered as important as the need to live together in harmony." "The life I now live ... I live by faith – by adherence to and reliance on and complete trust – in the Son of God, who loved me and gave himself up for me." Christ is not first in a class; he occupies the category all by himself.

For reading & meditation – Galatians 2:11-21

The last is the best

... he has spoken to us by his Son,
whom he appointed heir of all things ...
Hebrews 1:2

God's final Word to this world is in his Son. *That* is our claim as Christians. No other world faith claims that its great teacher was God incarnate. Yet we claim for Christ just that – and also that as God he meets every human need. He comes to us where we are and *he* does the work. He can relieve any plight of the human soul, and he has the power to meet every human need. Every spiritually sensitive person is aware of the presence of guilt which arises from indwelling sin, and is aware too that he or she alone can do nothing to dissolve it.

For reading & meditation – Hebrews 1:1-14

God incarnate

... He appeared in a body,
was vindicated by the Spirit ...
1 Timothy 3:16

Max Muller, a writer on religious issues, once made this arresting statement: "You do not know the worth of your Christian faith until you have compared it to others." The first article of belief we look at is the fact that God has appeared in this world in the Person of his eternal Son. Our faith is not the word of a prophet but the Word of the Son himself. No other world faith even attempts to represent its great teacher as God incarnate. Yet we claim for Christ just that. As God, he comes to us from the highest, and he comes all the way.

For reading & meditation – 1 Timothy 3:1-16

The Great Divide

The Word became flesh and made his dwelling among us.
John 1:14

The Son is as much God as God himself. "And the Word became flesh" (John 1:14). This verse has been described as "The Great Divide". Why "The Great Divide?" Because no other religion can claim that the word they received from God became flesh. In all other religions the essential element is a word become word – a philosophy, a moralistic system, and so on. Only in Christianity does God appear in human form; not a Word become word, but the Word become flesh. No other religion has anything like the Incarnation.

For reading & meditation – John 1:1-18

The thrilling truth

... but made himself nothing ...
being made in human likeness ...
Philippians 2:7

Religion is mankind's search for God; Christianity, however, is God's search for man. Therefore there are many religions, but only one gospel. Religion is the word become word; the gospel is the Word become flesh. John apparently could not get over the fact that God had become man in the Person of his Son, and sustained that thought throughout the whole of his writings. The Gospel unfolded the thrilling truth that the Son of God, became the Son of Man in order that the sons of men might become sons of God.

For reading & meditation – Philippians 2:1-11

God came himself

... God ... sent his one and only Son into the world that we might live through him.
1 John 4:9

Philosophy has strained itself to the utmost and yet it has not been successful in finding God. Moralism, likewise, cannot lead to God. The attempt to find God through the law was the noble effort made by the Jews. Never was such a moral system devised as was embodied by them, nor an end result so disappointing. It produced, for instance, the Pharisee who stood in his pride and said: "God, I thank you that I am not like other men" (Luke 18:11). They could not reach the kingdom by even their greatest self-effort alone. Both philosophy and moralism fall short.

For reading & meditation – 1 John 4:7-21

"I have Jesus Christ"

But when the time had fully come, God sent his Son ...
Galatians 4:4

The Christian faith is being attacked not only from outside but from within. The source of these attacks can be traced to those theological seminaries and training establishments which adopt a liberal approach to Christianity. Christ was not born of a virgin, they say, the miracles can be accounted for psychologically, and though Christ died on a cross his resurrection was not a physical one but a spiritual one. How sad that from so many pulpits one hears nothing more than a word become word.

For reading & meditation – Galatians 4:1-8

Shadow boxing

The law is only a shadow of the good things that are coming – not the realities themselves.
Hebrews 10:1

One day, after centuries of sacrificing animals – during which time God instilled in human minds the important idea of substitution – the unexpected happened. The writer to the Hebrews put it in these words: "Sacrifice and offering you did not desire, but a body you prepared for me" (v. 5). Christ said to the Father: "Here I am ... I have come to do your will." When the Son of God compressed himself into a human body, the greatest miracle of the ages took place. *This* was the substance; all else was shadow.

For reading & meditation – Hebrews 10:1-18

Attainment or obtainment?

... he is the beginning and the firstborn from among the dead ...
Colossians 1:18

"Does salvation come up from mankind through striving, helped by the Divine, or does it come down to us from above, through the act of God and our receptivity of that act? Is it an attainment or an obtainment?" That question separates Christianity from all other religions. The Christian faith teaches that salvation is the gift of God – obtainment, not attainment – Christianity alone falls into the category of obtainment. Christ is the meeting point of the human and the divine. No one else can hold that position.

For reading & meditation – Colossians 1:1-20

The genius of Christianity

... The virgin will be with child and will give birth to a son, and will call him Immanuel.
Isaiah 7:14

The Incarnation belongs to the very marrow of the gospel, therefore we can assert that God in the Person of his Son came to earth at a certain hour in history, lived and died among us, and afterwards rose from the dead. If people do not believe Christ's statements concerning himself and the reason why he came into this world then though they may be many splendid things they are not disciples of Christ. To be a Christian means first and foremost accepting the great fact of the Incarnation – that Christ, the second Person of the Trinity, was born at Bethlehem in the way the Scriptures describe.

For reading & meditation – Isaiah 7:13-17

Without a rival

From this time many of his disciples turned back and no longer followed him.
John 6:66

When Christ's followers started to drift away because he began to disappoint the hope they had of him, it seems the disciples started reconsidering their position too. Jesus knew what was going on in their minds and broke in on their thoughts with the question: "You do not want to leave too, do you?" John 6:67. Somehow that question seemed to clarify their minds. They saw in a flash his inevitability. They were shut up to Christ. Peter answered for them all: "To whom shall we go? You have the words of eternal life" (John 6:68).

For reading & meditation – John 6:60-71

Exposed realism

... he taught as one who had authority, and not as their teachers of the law.
Matthew 7:29

Jesus was teaching as One who had and was authority ... (Amplified Bible). What was this "authority"? An authority imposed from without? No, it was the authority of the facts. Jesus was divulging the meaning of life. He was uncovering reality. It was the authority of God; when *he* spoke God spoke. It was the authority of truth; when *he* spoke truth spoke. It was the authority of the deed; when *he* spoke, deed spoke. It was the authority of love; when *he* spoke, love spoke. Reality itself was speaking. Here was the indicative become the imperative.

For reading & meditation – Matthew 7:13-29

Good man or God-Man?

Can any of you prove me guilty of sin?
John 8:46

Jesus made the challenge: "Can any of you prove me guilty of sin?" The disciples had shared every kind of experience with him that mortals can share, yet they certainly could find no fault in him. Not only were his intimates unable to discover sin in him; he had no awareness of it in himself. He lived intimately with God his Father, but the holiness of God did not rebuke him. It didn't because it couldn't. He was sinless, spotless, perfect. Jesus is the God-Man.

For reading & meditation – John 8:31-47

"Not on trial"

I tell you that one greater than the temple is here.
Matthew 12:6

Jesus compared himself with the Temple's grandeur and significance and said: "I am greater than all this." It seemed preposterous. And yet the ages have vindicated him. The Temple is gone; all that is left is the Wailing Wall. Yet Christ lives on – and is the most potent power in human affairs. Jesus is bigger than every system whether it be religious, political or economic. They are related to him, not he to them. They must all stand before the judgment bar of his Person. Jesus is not just the greatest the world has ever seen; he is the greatest it will ever see.

For reading & meditation – Matthew 12:1-14

Lord and God

Thomas said to him, "My Lord and my God!"
John 20:28

The twelve disciples had been steeped in their high and ancient faith, and the belief in *one* God was firmly embedded in their minds. They were sure the Messiah, the Promised One, would come, but they hardly expected God to come himself, in Person, and in the garb of a working man. If Jesus was a good man but not God then when Thomas said, "My Lord and my God," he should have turned to Thomas and told him: "You can admire me but you must not worship me. I am not God." He didn't because he is God, and thus the right recipient of worship.

For reading & meditation – John 20:24-31

Greater than the Bible

You diligently study the Scriptures ...
These are the Scriptures that testify about me ...
John 5:39

Another claim that Jesus made which shows him to be not the least like any other person who has ever lived is his claim to be greater than the Scriptures. He did not emerge from the Bible, the Bible emerged from him. "There is one God and one mediator between God and men, the man Christ Jesus ..." (1 Tim. 2:5). It is true that we would know little of Christ were it not for the New Testament. But Christ existed before the New Testament. We honour the product but only as it leads us to Christ's feet and to an allegiance to him. Indeed, one greater than the Bible is here.

For reading & meditation – John 5:31-47

Our code is a Character

A new command I give you: Love one another. As I have loved you ...
John 13:34

What was new was this: "As I have loved you." Our Lord's conduct – "as I have loved you" – produced a new code for the human race. Paul catches the spirit of it when he says: "Treat one another with the same spirit as you experience in Christ Jesus" (Phil. 2:5). From the moment Jesus uttered the words there came into human life something more than a code – there came a Character. Our code is not a commandment but a Character. One greater than the Commandments is here.

For reading & meditation – John 13:1-38

Who can forgive?

... the Son of Man has authority on earth to forgive sins ...
Matthew 9:6

Perhaps one of the most significant ways in which Jesus is unlike anyone else who has ever lived is that he had the ability to forgive sins. There is one thing that not even the most highly trained team of psychoanalysts alone can do – they cannot *forgive*. They may expose an old wound, but they cannot heal it. They may show you that your trouble is an ancient sin, but they cannot cleanse it from the system. And that is what our sick souls need most of all – *forgiveness*. It's a lot easier to forgive yourself when you know that you yourself have been forgiven.

For reading & meditation – Matthew 9:1-12

That one solitary life

The men were amazed and asked,
"What kind of man is this?"
Matthew 8:27

Our Lord has no peers, no rivals and no successors. He is so different from every other leader, so unique, so superior, that he qualifies for a place on his own. The things he said about God are not the same as the sayings of any other religious teacher. The claims he made for himself are not ones that have been made by anyone else. His condemnation of human life and society goes deeper and is more devastating than that pronounced by any other man. The challenges and demands he made on his followers are more searching than those put forward by anyone – past and present.

For reading & meditation – Matthew 8:18-34

The God who seeks

Rejoice with me; I have found my lost sheep.
Luke 15:6

Christianity is essentially a rescue religion; it is the announcement of good news – the good news that God has come in the Person of his Son to save us from the power of sin, the penalty of sin, and one day in the future the presence of sin. God likens himself to a shepherd who leaves the rest of the sheep on their own in order to go after the one sheep that is lost. The Divine Shepherd, far from abandoning the sheep in the hope that, bleating and stumbling, it may find its own way home, puts his own life on the line to search it out.

For reading & meditation – Luke 15:1-10

The antechamber of faith

... Jesus said, "It is finished."
John 19:30

Christianity teaches that because we cannot save ourselves God came in the Person of his Son to do for us what we could not do for ourselves. Buddhism sees the main problem in life as suffering rather than sin, and the "desire" which is at the root of suffering. Deliverance comes through the abolition of desire by self-effort. Hinduism teaches the main problem in life is *maya* or *karma*, *maya* being illusion and *karma* retribution through reincarnation. From the endless cycle of rebirths or reincarnations there is no escape by forgiveness but only the final release of *nirvana*, involving the extinction of being. Salvation has been accomplished. It is ours to receive.

For reading & meditation – John 19:28-37

The way begins in a hole

... at just the right time, when we were still powerless, Christ died for the ungodly.
Romans 5:6

Why should the offer of free salvation in Christ be such a stumbling-block to the world? Mainly because it cuts deep into people's pride. The message of the gospel is this: there is simply nothing we can do to save ourselves. We must let God save us – or be lost. The moment we give up our pride and turn our face to God, confessing that we can do nothing to save ourselves, that moment we put ourselves in the position where we can be saved. The next step is simply to call out to the Lord and ask him to save you.

For reading & meditation – Romans 5:1-8

No change – no conversion

Greet ... Epenetus, who was the first convert to Christ in the province of Asia.
Romans 16:5

Salvation is the offer of divine forgiveness and the gift of eternal life; conversion is the way we enter into that experience and receive the gift. Jesus divided men and women into just two classes – the converted and the unconverted. Apparently, to him no other distinctions mattered. "*Except* ye be converted ... ye shall not enter into the kingdom of heaven." (Matthew 18:3). Conversion is the change by which one passes from the kingdom of self to the kingdom of God. And if there is no change there is no conversion.

For reading & meditation – Romans 16:1-16

Two types of conversion

... they told how the Gentiles had been converted. This news made all the brothers very glad.
Acts 15:3

Salvation is the word we use to describe the experience of our sins being forgiven and receiving the gift of eternal life. Conversion is the word we use to describe the way we enter into that experience. Sometimes non-Christian religions use the word conversion to describe a change of attitude in one of their adherents, but the change is always on the horizontal level rather than a vertical one. A change "on the horizontal" means a change on the human level, a change of thinking or approach, but not a change in relation to God – the vertical level. Conversion in Scripture is always vertical.

For reading & meditation – Acts 15:1-21

Vertical vs horizontal

... God, who is rich in mercy, made us alive with Christ even when we were dead in transgressions ...
Ephesians 2:4-5

A Hindu once said: "A man may change his acts but not his character." What he was saying was that a change is possible, but not a vertical change; there can be improvement, modification, a change of attitude, but no deep radical change. Many historians have called attention to the fact that when Christianity swept through Europe, there were many genuine conversions to Christ but many horizontal ones too – people taking the Name of Christ for political or economic expediency. They were converted horizontally but still in need of a vertical conversion.

For reading & meditation – Ephesians 2:1-10

Conversion – a miracle

... in Christ Jesus neither circumcision nor uncircumcision has any value.
Galatians 5:6

Conversion will involve a miraculous change; when it doesn't then it is not true conversion. What sort of change? There will be the slaying of the beast within, the gathering of the discordant forces of the soul into harmony, the cleansing of a stained conscience, entry into a more abundant life, and a deep inner sense of fellowship with Christ. Conversion doesn't have to be cataclysmic to be real either. The underlying facts are a new life, a new relationship. But it is as much a miracle as the calling forth of Lazarus from the dead.

For reading & meditation – Galatians 5:1-15

Bankruptcy confessed

... you were washed, you were sanctified, you were justified in the name of the Lord Jesus Christ ...
1 Corinthians 6:11

In his book Conversion – *Christian and Non-Christian*, the author, C. Underwood, says that the future of religion lies with the religions of the East, such as Hinduism and Buddhism, where conversions seem to occur. But the conversions he talks about are not the kind Jesus talked about. When people of any religion begin to become more interested in others than in themselves then that has to be applauded and recognised as beneficial. But that does not equate with the conversion talked about in the New Testament. When other helpers fail and comforts flee, there is always Jesus.

For reading & meditation – 1 Corinthians 6:1-11

"I know I'm saved"

... (Jesus) is able to save completely those who come to God through him ...
Hebrews 7:25

Is it possible to know without any shadow of doubt that one is saved and ready to meet God? Christianity says "Yes." Other religions are not sure and constantly express a note of uncertainty. Millions all over the world can say as Wesley did that they have an assurance they are saved and know that when they die they will go to heaven. It is not presumption to say you are saved providing, of course, you have entered into a personal relationship with Jesus Christ. Indeed, it is offensive for anyone who has given himself or herself to Christ *not* to say they are saved. Christ promises to save and save *completely*.

For reading & meditation – Hebrews 7:11-28

M.A. – Mightily Assured

... let us draw near to God with a sincere heart in full assurance of faith ...
Hebrews 10:22

The human heart longs for certainty – it needs to know without a shadow of doubt that the salvation of the soul is secure. The good news is that in Jesus Christ such security is found. When we turn from other religions to the Word of God it is like stepping out of thick fog into clear and brilliant sunlight. Faith is simply taking God at his Word, accepting what he asserts and acting accordingly. Listen to just one of the many things God says concerning this matter. "Everyone who calls on the name of the Lord will be saved". (Romans 10:13).

For reading & meditation – Hebrews 10:19-25

APRIL

Whose book is it?

All Scripture is God-breathed and is useful for teaching, correcting and training in righteousness ...
2 Timothy 3:16

Nearly every religion is based on a book. That is supremely true of the Christian religion. It too is based on a book, a holy book called the Bible. But the Bible is different from every other book, and is not only different but absolutely unique. Like the One about whom it speaks, it is in a category all by itself. It is unique because of its Author. God is its Author. With other books you have to understand the book in order to know the author. With the Bible you have to know the Author in order to understand the book.

For reading & meditation – 2 Timothy 3:10-17

A Father's pleasure

And a voice came from heaven:
"You are my Son, whom I love ..."
Mark 1:11

What strikes as strange about the sacred books of other religions that purport to have come from God is that they have no reference to the plan of salvation as brought to us by the Lord Jesus Christ. The main theme of the Bible is Christ. All the Old Testament truths converge on him and all the New Testament truths emerge from him. "This is my Son whom I love and with whom I am well pleased." If God is so excited about his Son, why is it that in the sacred books of other religions (said to come direct from God) there is no mention of him?

For reading & meditation – Mark 1:1-12

A God who has no Son ...

For God so loved the world that
he gave his one and only Son ...
John 3:16

It seems strange that God should have so much to say about his Son in the Bible and yet ignore him when supposedly revealing himself to the founders of other religions. The main difference between Islam and Christianity is that God (Allah) has no Son. A God who has no Son has to rely on intermediaries to bring people to himself. And an intermediary who is not God and not man cannot effect complete reconciliation. It would be like a wonderfully constructed bridge but broken at the farther end.

For reading & meditation – John 3:1-17

"Before all worlds"

Jesus said ... "I am returning to my Father and your Father, to my God and your God."
John 20:17

To beget is to become the father of; to create is to make. When you beget, you beget something of the same kind as yourself. What God begets is God, just as what man begets is man. That is why human beings are not sons of God in the sense that Christ is. They may be like God in certain ways, but they are not of the same kind. One of the creeds says that Christ is the Son of God, "begotten not created", and adds: "begotten by his Father before all worlds." "Before all worlds." Christ is begotten, not created. For what purpose? That you and I might have a Divine Father also.

For reading & meditation – John 20:10-18

In all the Scriptures!

Were not our hearts burning ... while he talked with us ... and opened the Scriptures to us?
Luke 24:32

The Scriptures were written over a period of some fifteen hundred years by about forty different penmen, and yet although of such composite character, the book displays an amazing and essential unity. The most wonderful thing about the written Word is that woven through it from end to end, like a golden thread, the *living* Word can be observed. Those forty different authors did not know when they were writing that they were putting together a book that tells us as no other the full story of the Lord Jesus Christ.

For reading & meditation – Luke 24:13-35

The book of books

The grass withers and the flowers fall,
but the word of our God stands for ever.
Isaiah 40:8

Large sections of the Bible were personally dictated to men by God, the Ten Commandments being just one example. The writers of the Bible were, divinely indemnified against errors of observation, lapses of memory and unintentional misrepresentations of facts. Their writings were honest, accurate, and supervised by the Holy Spirit before being compiled into this wonderful book we call the Bible. No wonder it is often referred to as the "book of books".

For reading & meditation – Isaiah 40:1-11

God's great masterpiece

All Scripture is God breathed ...
2 Timothy 3:16

God led the minds and hearts of the writers of Scripture to go to the right sources for information, to come up with the required data, and in the process protected them from exposure to error, deceit or imposture. He supervised them in their research, in their reporting, and when he spoke directly to them he was there also to make sure that they received clearly the message he wanted to convey. Who wrote the Bible? Moses, David, Isaiah, Jeremiah, John, Peter, Paul, and many others. But whose book is it really? It is God's.

For reading & meditation – Psalm 132:1-18

The unique cross

For the message of the cross is foolishness to those who are perishing ...
1 Corinthians 1:18

The cross humbles all pride and dashes all hope of self-salvation. It also speaks of the tremendous and uncalculating generosity of God in providing for us a salvation that is without price. The chapters of the *Qur'an* do not tell of a costly and historic display of God's mercy as portrayed by the cross and spoken of in each of the four Gospels. In Islam, Allah is merciful to the meritorious, those who pray, give alms and fast in Ramadan. In Christianity God is merciful to sinners not because of their good works but because of Christ's sacrifice for them on the cross.

For reading & meditation – 1 Corinthians 1:18-31

The key to life

*May I never boast except in the cross
of our Lord Jesus Christ ...*
Galatians 6:14

Whenever a person says that all religions are the same, a person's mind runs immediately to the cross. No authentic note of divine self-sacrifice comes from other faiths. The cross stands out in absolute uniqueness. Christ's cross is the only true key to life. This and this alone unlocks the doors to some of life's greatest mysteries. Other religions try, sometimes with great sincerity, to unlock the doors to these profound mysteries, but they are unsuccessful because they do not have the right key. They do not have a cross.

For reading & meditation – Galatians 6:1-18

Understanding the cross

But God demonstrates his own love for us in this: While we were still sinners, Christ died for us.
Romans 5:8

We will never in our mortal state be able to grasp the full meaning of the cross. But what we do grasp gives us a clue to what lies in the heart of the Infinite. The most vital approach to the cross is not through a theory but through an attitude of mind and heart that responds to its meaning. To understand the cross one must have a sacrificial spirit within one. Those who profess to know Christ but live only for self will know something of the cross but will miss its real meaning. The cross is best understood not by an argument but by an attitude.

For reading & meditation – Romans 5:6-21

One long search for God

For from within, out of men's hearts, come evil thoughts ...
Mark 7:21

The history of humanity is "one long search for God". We long for fellowship with God. Yet something dark, dreadful and sinister stands between us and God. We realise God is pure, and because we are conscious of our impurity we hardly dare ask for fellowship with him. We are separated and guilty. The object of all religions is to bring those who long for fellowship with God into correspondence with him. But how is that achieved? Christianity says it can be done only through the cross. Other religions point to other ways, and claim their way is as valid as the Christian way. God says the cross is the only way.

For reading & meditation – Mark 7:8-23

At-one-ment

God presented him as a sacrifice of atonement, through faith in his blood.
Romans 3:25

"The task of religion is at-one-ment: atonement. If it fails to do this it fails at the vital point." The wonderful distinctive of Christianity is this – Jesus Christ has done something about the problem of being out of correspondence with God. He puts the hand of a penitent sinner into the hand of a pardoning God. To deliver men and women from evil was a problem that challenged God's power and made the deepest claim upon his love. The cross is the answer. If we don't take God's way of salvation then nothing else will do.

For reading & meditation – Romans 3:21-31

An unintentional tribute

"He saved others," they said,
"but he can't save himself!"
Matthew 27:42

The crowd who watched Jesus cried: "He saved others, but he can't save himself!" But strange as it seems, that mocking phrase became the central truth of the gospel. *He was saving others and therefore he could not save himself.* This law of saving by self-giving runs through life. Those who save themselves cannot save others, and those who save others cannot save themselves – cannot save themselves trouble, sorrow, hurts, disappointments, pain and sometimes even death. This is a law of the universe, and applies to God as much as it does to us.

For reading & meditation – Matthew 27:32-44

The ultimate discovery

... when the centurion ... saw how he died, he said, "Surely this man was the Son of God!"
Mark 15:39

God would not write a law of "saving by sacrifice" within our hearts and evade it himself. The cross spells out the message that God is prepared to take into himself the suffering caused by sin and, indeed, to take on himself the very sins of the ones he created. No other religion can conceive of such a thing. The cross raised on Calvary is but a reflection of an inner cross lying in the heart of God. Through it we see that at the centre of the universe is redeeming love. No greater discovery could be made or will be made than that – in earth or in heaven. It is the ultimate in discoveries.

For reading & meditation – Mark 15:16-39

A sacrificial Head

For whoever wants to save his life will lose it, but whoever loses his life for me will save it.
Luke 9:24

The spirit of self-giving is the most beautiful thing in life. Through it life rises to the highest level. When the sacrificial spirit is absent from life, that life is of the lowest kind; where it is partially developed that life is higher. Where it is perfectly embodied, that life is highest on the scale of being. If this law holds true on earth but is reversed in relation to God then laws are meaningless and the universe is without a Head. But such is not the case. God is not a disappointment. The cross shouts out to all who will hear that the universe has a sacrificial Head.

For reading & meditation – Luke 9:18-27

APRIL 15

The Man of Galilee

For what I received I passed on to you as of first importance ... that he was raised on the third day ...
1 Corinthians 15:3-4

There is no more glorious event in the Christian calendar than Easter Day. This is the day on which we celebrate our Lord's rising from the dead. What other world religion has at its heart such a glorious fact? Christianity is the only faith whose Founder died upon a cross, was buried for three days, and then returned from the dead. There are voices in today's Church trying to persuade us that the resurrection of Christ never took place – that our Lord did not rise from the dead in bodily form.

For reading & meditation – 1 Corinthians 15:1-11

A basic precondition

They still did not understand from Scripture that Jesus had to rise from the dead.
John 20:9

"If you confess with your mouth, 'Jesus is Lord,' and believe ... *that God raised him from the dead*, you will be saved" (Romans 10:9). Here Paul makes it crystal clear that acceptance of the fact that Christ rose from the dead is a basic precondition for being a Christian. It was not just the spiritual part of Jesus that continued after the tomb – it was the total Christ. "See my hands," he said to doubting Thomas, "put (your hand) into my side ... and believe" (John 20:27). Our Lord's resurrection was a physical one. If it wasn't then there is no salvation.

For reading & meditation – John 20:1-18

"The Swoon Theory"

God has raised this Jesus to life,
and we are all witnesses of the fact.
Acts 2:32

Clearly our Lord *actually* died. The Gospels provide us with medical evidence for the fact. One of the soldiers pierced his side and there came forth "blood and water". Was it really a convalescent Christ the disciples encountered on that first Easter Day? No, the Master, as it were, had flung from his face the mask of death, and laid down in the hearts and minds of his disciples an impression that stayed with them throughout the whole of their ministry. He who had been dead was now alive – gloriously and resplendently.

For reading & meditation – Acts 2:29-41

The true and the false

... our Saviour, Christ Jesus ... has destroyed death and has brought life and immortality to light ...
2 Timothy 1:10

When we talk about Christ's resurrection, we are not saying he survives in our memories. Recollection is not resurrection. This is what is meant by our Lord's resurrection: the body which died upon the cross and was laid in the cool tomb on the evening of the first Good Friday was miraculously infused with life once again early in the morning of the first Easter Day. It is as literal and as factual as that. This – nothing less and nothing else – is what we mean by the resurrection of our Lord from the dead.

For reading & meditation – 2 Timothy 1:1-18

The mystery rolled back

Where, O death, is your victory?
Where, O death, is your sting?
1 Corinthians 15:55

Death is a mystery – "the undiscovered country from which no traveller returns". Then came the first Easter Day, and the stone was rolled away. One Traveller did return. Death is an abysmal cavern no longer but a tunnel with light at the farther end. If men and women have seen it as a blind alley then they need think no longer in those terms. It is now a thoroughfare, a highway. "Tis death is dead, not he." The mystery is a mystery no more. The stone that was rolled away the first Easter morn was not just the rock that sealed the tomb. Our Lord rolled back for us the mystery of death also.

For reading & meditation – 1 Corinthians 15:50-58

Not an exit – an entrance

... an angel of the Lord ... going
to the tomb, rolled back the stone ...
Matthew 28:2

The stone was rolled away not that our Lord might come out but that the disciples might go in. It was intended not as a means of exit but as a means of entrance. "God rolled away the stone not that his Son might rise, but that we might know he had risen; that we might steal into the empty tomb and see only the place where they laid him." That is why God rolled away the stone. It was not necessary for the resurrection, but it was necessary for its proclamation.

For reading & meditation – Matthew 28:1-15

A glorious uprising

... You will not let your Holy One see decay.
Acts 13:35

Peter saw "the strips of linen lying there, as well as the burial cloth that had been around Jesus' head" (John 20:6). There was no possibility that the graveclothes could have looked the way they did without a resurrection. Had the head-cloth been torn apart, the impression gained would have been quite different. It was probably this simple but tremendous fact – the fact that Jesus had clearly passed through the shroud without it being unwound – that convinced the first observer they had witnessed the miracle of resurrection.

For reading & meditation – Acts 13:16-41

Ante-room to glory

... he raised [Christ] from the dead and seated him at his right hand in the heavenly realms ...
Ephesians 1:20

First, *the resurrection of Christ assures us of God's forgiveness*. The resurrection is convincing proof that Christ's sacrifice on the cross was accepted, and thus gives us the assurance that all our sins can be forgiven. Second, *the resurrection of Christ assures us of God's power*. It is one thing to be forgiven, it is another to live above the power of sin. God can change people's character. Third, *the resurrection assures us of God's ultimate triumph*. Other religions and ideologies have vague ideas about the future. Death for a believer is nothing more than the ante-room to glory.

For reading & meditation – Ephesians 1:15-23

Risen ... and exalted

... he was taken up before their very eyes, and a cloud hid him from their sight.
Acts 1:9

"It is not 'Christianity' as an empirical institution or system for which Christians should claim superiority. It is Christ, and only Christ. We should not be afraid to affirm without embarrassment that Christ is superior to all other religious leaders, precisely because he alone humbled himself in love even to the cross and therefore God has raised him 'above' every other person, rank, or title." If God has given this supreme position to Jesus and so honoured him then we should give him the same honour also.

For reading & meditation – Acts 1:1-11

No cross without a crown

He ... ascended higher than all the heavens, in order to fill the whole universe.
Ephesians 4:10

The cross is not complete without the crown. The ascension inevitably followed the atonement; the coronation the crucifixion. One modern-day writer says: "One senses a certain embarrassment in some ministers where the subject of the Ascension is concerned. They tend to shy clear of the topic or dismiss it lightly as no more than a graphic myth or triumphalist parable." But if there had been no ascension there would be no gospel. The cross would not be complete without the crown.

For reading & meditation – Ephesians 4:1-16

Christ – our Precursor

... Jesus, who went before us ...
Hebrews 6:20

Out of all the aspects of truth that surround the fact of our Lord's ascension, one of the greatest is surely this – Christ is our Precursor. A precursor is a forerunner. "Forerunner" brings to mind a picture of our Lord as a celestial outrider "bringing many sons to glory" (Heb. 2:10), and reminds us of a petition in the great high priestly prayer: "Father, I want those you have given me to be with me where I am, and to see my glory ..." (John 17:24). Whatever the future holds for us, we who are Christ's can be sure of this: our Lord has ascended into heaven. And so, too, shall we.

For reading & meditation – Hebrews 6:1-20

"Jesus, Yes – Church, No"

We implore you on Christ's behalf:
Be reconciled to God.
2 Corinthians 5:20

Being Christians does not mean we therefore have to believe that all other religions are wrong through and through. While never budging from what we believe, we must show a loving disposition towards those of other faiths. We can be passionate in our faith without being discourteous to people. We may disagree with what someone believes, but we must disagree agreeably. As one old preacher quaintly put it: "To win some we must be winsome."

For reading & meditation – 2 Corinthians 5:11-21

"Common grace"

For in him we live and move and have our being.
Acts 17:28

God is active not only in the Church but in the world and in those belonging to other religions also. "He is not far from each one of us" (Acts 17:27). "Common grace" is the kindness God shows to all human beings even though they know him not. This is not to be confused with "saving grace", which is the kindness *and* mercy he extends to those who humbly receive the sacrificial offering which his Son made for them on the cross. There is no better way to end a discussion with an adherent of some other faith than to say and mean: "God loves you, and so do I."

For reading & meditation – Acts 17:16-34

Three important facts

Now we are all here ... to listen to everything the Lord has commanded you to tell us.
Acts 10:33

There is no such thing as self-salvation. Nobody can achieve salvation by his or her religion, sincerity, or good works. Second, Jesus Christ is the only way to God and the only Saviour. Our Lord himself said: "No-one comes to the Father except through me". Third, we do not know how much knowledge and understanding of the gospel a person needs to have in order to call upon God for mercy and be saved. He will work for those who are willing to give up all ideas of saving themselves and look to him alone for salvation.

For reading & meditation – Acts 10:23-48

In conclusion

No-one comes to the Father except through me.
John 14:6

Christianity is unique. It is unique in the sense that it is the divinely appointed way to enter into a relationship with the one true and living God. There is only one way, only one Name, only one God, only one Lord, only one Mediator. And it is precisely because Jesus Christ is the *only* Saviour that we are under an obligation to proclaim him to as many as we possibly can. In whatever culture we live, we must endeavour to make Jesus known. *No true Christian can ever worship Christ without minding that others do not.*

For reading & meditation – John 14:1-14

MAY

A Counsellor par excellence

... I will ask the Father, and I will give you another Counsellor to be with you for ever ...
John 14:16

The Spirit came, as we know, at Pentecost, to be to the disciples all that Jesus was – and more. And he has remained in the world to be our Counsellor too. But how dependent are we on his counsel? How often do we draw on his resources? Sadly, all too seldom and too little. God has appointed a divine Counsellor to assist us, yet so often we prefer to muddle along on our own.

For reading & meditation – John 14:1-17

A permanent presence

I will not leave you as orphans; I will come to you.
John 14:18

When the Holy Spirit visited them at Pentecost the dispirited disciples came alive again, and appeared to become twice the men they were when Jesus was with them. Why? The answer is quite simple. Jesus had been *with* them, but the Holy Spirit was *in* them and would remain *in* them. There was no fear that he might go away. He would remain with them always. And what he was to them he is to us also – a permanent presence.

For reading & meditation – John 14:18-31

Glorious foreverness

... The man on whom you see the Spirit come down and remain ... will baptise with the Holy Spirit.
John 1:33

The words *and remain* and the phrase used in John 14:16 – *to be with you for ever* – strike the same note. The idea of an occasional visitation is replaced by a permanent coming. The Holy Spirit is a Counsellor who is available every day and all day. You can approach him any time of night or day, and though he may be involved at the same time in counselling thousands of your fellow believers, he will give himself to you as if you were the only one on the face of the planet. And you don't have to look for him in any other place than in your own heart.

For reading & meditation – John 1:19-34

Another Counsellor

Paul ... travelled throughout ... Phrygia ... having been kept by the Holy Spirit from preaching ... in the province of Asia.
Acts 16:6

"Holy Spirit" and "Spirit of Jesus" are used interchangeably – "having been kept by the Holy Spirit from preaching the word" (Acts 16:6), and "the Spirit of Jesus would not allow them to" (Acts 16:7). The Holy Spirit seemed to the disciples to be the Spirit of Jesus within them. They were one. The counsel given to every believer by the Holy Spirit will accord with the counsel given to the disciples by Jesus when he was here on earth. If God is a Christlike God, then the Spirit is a Christlike Spirit.

For reading & meditation – Acts 16:1-10

The first thing

If any of you lacks wisdom, he should ask God ...
James 1:5

The *first* thing we should do whenever we have a problem that cannot be solved using our own resources is to turn to the divine Counsellor and invite him to help us. If light does not come *then* seek the help of a wise and godly friend. But seeking help from others should not be our first recourse; our first recourse should be to God. The Holy Spirit is a Counsellor *par excellence*. To seek counselling from another Christian is, of course, quite valid, but that kind of counselling might be needed less if we depended on the Holy Spirit more.

For reading & meditation – James 1:1-11

Grief in the Godhead

And do not grieve the Holy Spirit of God ...
Ephesians 4:30

We are in the midst of what is being called a "counselling explosion", and are in danger of falling into the trap of taking our problems first to a Christian counsellor rather than bringing them straight to God. If you are a Christian then his resources are available to you – free and for the taking. God and Christ do for you, as one of his children, what any good government will do; they provide you with counsel. When we spurn the services of the divine Counsellor we grieve him. For he is not merely an influence; he is a *Person*.

For reading & meditation – Ephesians 4:17-32

"He" – not "it"

... the Holy Spirit said, "Set apart for me Barnabas and Saul ..."
Acts 13:2

The Holy Spirit is not merely an influence but a divine *Person*. This is why we must refer to him as "he" and not "it". He is a Person in the same way that you and I are persons – only of course much more so. The Bible says he is God, with the very same attributes as God. In Job 26:13 he is seen as having the power to create. In Psalm 139:7 he is shown to have omnipresence – being everywhere present. In Hebrews 3:7 he is spoken of as issuing commands – something only God can do. And in 2 Corinthians 3:17 he is referred to as "Lord".

For reading & meditation – Acts 13:1-12

Who is the real you?

What a wretched man I am! Who will rescue me from this body of death?
Romans 7:24

To whom do we refer when we describe ourselves by the personal pronoun "I"? In our personalities is there anything so constant and reliable that we can honestly refer to it as "I"? The same person can be so many different persons. Whom do others mean when they say "you", and whom do you mean when you say "I"? The real "you" is not the person others see, not even the person you see, but the person God, Christ and the Holy Spirit see.

For reading & meditation – Romans 7:7-25

Double vision

Jesus ... said, "You are Simon son of John. You will be called Cephas" (which ... is Peter).
John 1:42

One of the characteristics of a good counsellor is to have a clear vision of a person's potential so that they can encourage that person to move towards it. Jesus looked at Simon and declared: "You are Simon ... You will be called Cephas (which ... is Peter). He was saying that he saw within Peter the potential to be a rock, for that is what the name "Peter" means. The Holy Spirit sees us as we are, loves us as we are, but yet loves us too much to let us stay as we are. Lovingly and gently he prods us towards perfection.

For reading & meditation – John 1:35-42

How many Simons?

... and you have been given fullness in Christ, who is head over every power and authority.
Colossians 2:10

We never see ourselves as others see us. Indeed, we do not even see ourselves as others see us *physically*. When we look in a mirror the image we see is always reversed. And mentally and spiritually it is the same; it is another self we see from within. To see ourselves as others see us may be helpful, but what is more helpful is to see ourselves as God, Christ and the Holy Spirit see us. They see us not merely as we are, with dark marks on our soul, but as we can be – complete in the Godhead.

For reading & meditation – Colossians 2:1-11

False self-images

... Simon's mother-in-law was suffering from a high fever, and they asked Jesus to help her.
Luke 4:38

We never see ourselves as we really are. Simon appeared to have a great concern when his mother-in-law was ill. If someone had said to Simon "Are you without fault?", he might have answered: "No, I do have some faults." But he wouldn't have particularised them. Usually people don't until they are serious in the pursuit of holiness. Then, and only then, will we dig them out, itemise them, pray over them and say: "This, and this, and this is sin within me."

For reading & meditation – Luke 4:38-44

A reed turns into a rock

See, I lay a stone in Zion, a
chosen and precious cornerstone ...
1 Peter 2:6

Through the combination of Christ's counselling and later the Holy Spirit's counselling, Peter became clear in judgment and firm in will. "The man who could curse and swear and deny all knowledge of his best friend to save his own skin became a valiant leader at Pentecost and the unshaken champion of the sect which was itself to change the world." Peter had taken on the characteristics of his Lord which were foreign to his own nature. "This is what I will make of you," Jesus had said, "a rock." And he did.

For reading & meditation – 1 Peter 2:1-10

Divine enticement

No longer will you be called Abram;
your name will be Abraham ...
Genesis 17:5

Our Lord's dealings with Simon Peter, particularly in respect of putting before him a vision of what he could be, set a pattern the Holy Spirit follows in his counselling ministry with us. Have you ever been at prayer and caught a vision, if only for a moment, of what it would mean to be the person you longed to be? That was the ministry of the divine Counsellor at work within you. He sees with double vision, and to get more of that double vision we must determine to spend more time with him.

For reading & meditation – Genesis 17:1-15

Confined in a cage!

God said to him, "Your name is Jacob, but you will no longer be called Jacob; your name will be Israel."
Genesis 35:10

Just as Jesus looked on Simon the reed and saw Peter the rock, so the Holy Spirit looks on you and sees you maybe as ineffective, beaten, cowed and fearful, but he also sees you as confident, effective, sanctified, and strong, moving ahead along the Christian pathway with great strides. If only we could move closer to him, stand at his side and get that double vision – the vision of the men and women we are and the men and women we might be. But what stops us getting close? Mainly it is our unwillingness. When our *will* is intent on getting closer, we *will* find a way.

For reading & meditation – Genesis 35:1-15

The person God meant

And we ... are being transformed into his likeness with ever-increasing glory ...
2 Corinthians 3:18

Many of us keep the Holy Spirit at a safe distance. "Explaining the Holy Spirit is one thing; experiencing him another." The Holy Spirit yearns to transform us in the same way that Christ yearned to transform Simon Peter. It means taking time to develop our relationship with him. Once we do that, however, he goes to work, inflaming, enlightening, prodding, enticing, and moving us on until the difference in us is so marked that we need a new name.

For reading & meditation – 2 Corinthians 3:7-18

No prayer – no power

... Jesus told his disciples a parable to show them that they should always pray and not give up.
Luke 18:1

Jesus seeks constantly to set before us an image of the man or woman he sees us to be, and the more we give ourselves to him the more he can give himself to us. Often when people are overcome by troubles and trials they find it difficult to pray. It's not easy to pray when things all around us are falling apart, but hard though it may be to accept, that is the time we ought to pray the most. Indeed, one of the goals of a godly counsellor is to help a person get back to a consistent prayer life, for without one there is little chance of spiritual survival. If we do not pray, we faint.

For reading & meditation – Luke 18:1-8

Running from the crowds!

But Jesus often withdrew to lonely places and prayed.
Luke 5:16

Why did Jesus spend so much time counselling his disciples to pray? Because prayer opens us to God and to the resources of the Holy Spirit. When we are in touch with God through prayer then the Holy Spirit supplies the energy we need to get through every day. Our Lord is the perfect example of a Counsellor who practised what He preached. On many occasions He escaped from the crowds to pray. Christ ran away from the multitudes to get alone and pray. That shows how much of a priority our Lord gave to prayer. Jesus needed to pray. So do we.

For reading & meditation – Luke 5:12-15

Pray! Pray! Pray!

... pray continually ...
1 Thessalonians 5:17

Put quite simply, prayer is the heart of our faith. Over the years people have asked these questions: "What is the heart of Christian living? How do I grow in grace and power?" Prayer is the way. Many of our ideas concerning prayer are confused, and many find it difficult to pray, even when no problems are crowding into their lives. Some people pray only when they want something. You may have heard of the little boy who told his vicar that he didn't pray everday because there were some days when he didn't want anything. What would you think of a friend who turned up only when he wanted something?

For reading & meditation – 1 Thessalonians 5:1-23

When disinclined to pray

And pray in the Spirit on all occasions with all kinds of prayers and requests.
Ephesians 6:18

But even those who see prayer as more than asking for things often find it difficult to pray. The need for prayer is apparent, the command to pray is recognised, but the *longing* to pray is not in them. They have to push themselves to get down on their knees. What a tragedy. Thankfully, the divine Counsellor is willing to come to our aid. Paul says (Rom. 8:26): "The Spirit helps us in our weaknesses." And never is the Holy Spirit more helpful than when he helps us pray.

For reading & meditation – Ephesians 6:10-20

"The Spirit is praying!"

... the Spirit himself intercedes for us
with groans that words cannot express.
Romans 8:26

Sometimes our divine Counsellor, knowing that prayer brings about God's redemptive purposes, takes up the task of intercession for us "with groans that words cannot express". The sighs of the Spirit are clearly interpreted by God, because it is for God's own purpose for each one of us that the Spirit is pleading. It is always an awesome moment when one senses that one is being prayed *through*. All one can do is to silence every other voice that rises up in the soul and say: "Hush! The Holy Spirit is praying!"

For reading & meditation – Romans 8:18-27

The groan of God

... Jesus ... was deeply moved in spirit and troubled.
John 11:33

Progress in spiritual things is not mechanical. It does not come from ourselves alone. Progress results from the groan of God in the hearts of his people. Was the groan that Jesus felt as he confronted death God groaning within him? Was it the spiritual precursor of something mighty and momentous? If it is true that "all true progress in this world is by the echo of the groan of God in the hearts of his people", then ought we not to ask ourselves: When did we last feel the groan of God in our soul?

For reading & meditation – John 11:32-44

MAY 21

Three groans!

For while we are in this tent,
we groan and are burdened ...
2 Corinthians 5:4

First *the whole creation groans*. Everything that lives is subject to disease: human beings, animals, fish, birds, trees, plants. Second, *we groan within ourselves*. "We have not progressed very far in the Christian life if we have not felt the groan that goes on in creation ... and felt also the groan in our own hearts – the longing to be released from bondage and be with *Christ*." Third, and most astonishing of all, *the Spirit groans within us*. But know this also: God's last word is not a groan. God's *last* word is joy, joy, joy!

For reading & meditation – 2 Corinthians 5:1-10

Face to face with reality

Jesus said to her, "You are right when you say you have no husband."
John 4:17

Another aspect of good counselling, and one which we see demonstrated both by our Lord and the Holy Spirit, is bringing important issues to a head through *loving confrontation*. This involves moving people away from symptoms on the surface to face the significant issues. Christ demonstrated this skill in his encounter with the woman at the well. He pinpointed her problem in a delicate way: "Go, call your husband" (v. 16). She replied weakly: "I have no husband." Christ always saw past the trivial issues to the major ones, and never hesitated, though always respectfully, to bring the hidden things to light.

For reading & meditation – John 4:1-26

Handle with care!

Brothers, if someone is caught in a sin, you who are spiritual should restore him gently.
Galatians 6:1

If it is true that in almost every life there is "an issue which needs confronting", then what is to be done about it? It must be faced and faced courageously. There is a form of Christian counselling known as "nouthetic counselling", *noutheteo* being the Greek word for to warn, admonish, confront. Some of its practitioners appear to be more interested in exposing sin than restoring the sinner. Where there is moral failure, it is restoration, not exposure, that ought to be the overriding consideration. To confront does not mean to affront.

For reading & meditation – Galatians 6:1-10

The arguments of sin

... but each one is tempted when, by his own evil desire, he is dragged away and enticed.
James 1:14

One day you find yourself being tempted by something that hitherto you have always resisted. But this time you begin to look at it a little differently. Perhaps you begin to talk to yourself like this: "The pressures in my life at the moment are so strong that surely a little escape from them can be justified. After all, the world is not a Sunday school. No one can blame me for just one lapse – just one." This is called "the rationalisation of desire" or the *arguments* of sin.

For reading & meditation – James 1:12-18

David's great sin

But the thing David had done displeased the Lord.
2 Samuel 11:27

King David knew all about "the rationalisation of desire". He wanted the wife of Uriah, one of his officers, and while Uriah was on active service fighting the king's battles, David seduced the woman. David was so self-deceived that on this occasion even the Holy Spirit was unable to get through to him (he will plead but never overpower), and so the Spirit used Nathan as one of his "temporary assistants". Nathan's barbed little parable did its work. Soon the wail of the Psalm 51 arose: "Have mercy on me, O God ... wash me, and I shall be whiter than snow" (Psa. 51:1, 7).

For reading & meditation – 2 Samuel 11:1-27

He is always there!

... you were marked in him with a seal, the promised Holy Spirit ... guaranteeing our inheritance ...
Ephesians 1:13

Does the Spirit withdraw from our hearts if we ever fall into sin? He is hurt by our sin, even grieved by it, but he remains with us and in us nevertheless. Some would *like* to believe that he *does* leave when we fall into sin, for the thought of a grieved and hurting Spirit residing in the soul greatly increases their spiritual discomfort. He will not desert you. You may grieve him and turn a deaf ear to him, and if you do not heed him it is possible that his voice may grow faint within you. We are sealed by the Spirit until the day of redemption. *He is always there.*

For reading & meditation – Ephesians 1:1-14

The purifying Spirit

(The Holy Spirit) purified their hearts by faith.
Acts 15:9

Christians are in danger of being brainwashed by the world into lowering our moral standards. This attitude must not be allowed to invade the Church. During a TV panel programme one person objected to the low standards being accepted everywhere today. A member of the panel retorted: "But it's only human nature." That sums up the spirit of the world: "It's nature and therefore hardly sin." We must never forget that the Spirit's *greatest* work is helping us to be cleansed from sin and to overcome sin. He is, we must always remember, the *Holy* Spirit.

For reading & meditation – Acts 15:1-11

Sensitivity to sin

If we claim to be without sin, we deceive ourselves ...
1 John 1:8

Today we ask ourselves: Is a sense of sin old-fashioned? Our fathers used to talk a lot about the way the Holy Spirit convicted of sin, but "conviction of sin" is a phrase we don't use much nowadays. Let us be on our guard lest in our unwillingness to express ourselves in the self-depreciating language of our fathers we grow smug in our attitude to sin. It is perilously possible that without realising it we may have been affected by the tendency of this age to reduce the eternal distinction between right and wrong to a question of taste.

For reading & meditation – 1 John 1:1-10

The scrutiny of God

Search me, O God, and know my heart ...
Psalm 139:23

Spiritual examination ought to be a regular activity. The whole purpose of self-examination is to indentify the things that should not be in our lives and to bring them to God so that they may be uprooted. The Spirit never moves us to self-pity; the Spirit moves us to repentance. Self-pity is an enemy of repentance because it is an attempt to remove the soul's pain by humanistic means rather than by entrusting oneself to God and his Holy Spirit. "Search me, O God ... See if there is any offensive way in me" (vv. 23-24).

For reading & meditation – Psalm 139:1-24

Whose voice was it?

You ... are controlled not by the sinful nature but by the Spirit, if the Spirit of God lives in you.
Romans 8:9

The Holy Spirit, our divine Counsellor, is at work within our hearts pleading against the arguments of sin. He, like our Lord, never hesitates to make us aware of important issues in our hearts, but he does so in the same way that Jesus did – tenderly, delicately and respectfully. What if, when the arguments of sin arose, he had left us without a word? It doesn't bear thinking about. Jesus loved people enough to plead with them to give up their sin. The Holy Spirit does so too.

For reading & meditation – Romans 8:1-11

JUNE

A piercing question

"You do not want to leave too, do you?" Jesus asked the Twelve.
John 6:67

"You do not want to leave too, do you?" Our Lord's question probably caused the disciples' minds to range far and wide. Who would replace Jesus? Where could one find a satisfactory alternative? Reflectively and with painstaking care Peter considered the possibilities. The Saviour's dramatic question had put the whole issue into clear perspective. Peter's reply was magnificent: "Lord, to whom shall we go? You have the words of eternal life." The Master's piercing question had left them in no doubt about the direction in which they should go.

For reading & meditation – John 6:60-70

Light for the way ahead

You guide me with your counsel ...
Psalm 73:24

"He," said Jesus, speaking of the Holy Spirit, "will guide you into all truth" (John 16:13). It is the Spirit who helps to clarify the issues that puzzle us and assists us in seeing clearly the next step we must take. Without weakening our personalities and thus making us overly dependent, the divine Counsellor remains at hand to bring clarity and illumination to our minds whenever we need it. That guidance, of course, comes in different ways – through Scripture, through circumstances, through sanctified reasoning or through the Spirit speaking directly to our hearts.

For reading & meditation – Psalm 73:1-28

A sense of being led

... those who are led by the Spirit
of God are sons of God.
Romans 8:14

Every one of us if we are to be at our best must have a sense of instrumentation, of being guided by our God, of fulfilling a will that is ultimate. Much of our life may be lacking direction and goals. If we lose the sense of being led by the Spirit we become victims of our circumstances. Then we are circumstance-directed instead of Spirit-directed. Guidance by the Holy Spirit is the very essence of Christianity. If there is no sense of leadership we will have no sense of sonship. We simply must have a sense of being led.

For reading & meditation – Romans 8:12-17

God where it counts

All of them were filled with the Holy Spirit ...
Acts 2:4

There is a great debate among theologians as to whether the last twelve verses of Mark's Gospel are part of his original text. Some say they were added by a later writer. If this is so then Mark's Gospel ends with the words of chapter 16 verse 8: "They said nothing to anyone, because they were afraid." Such was not the case, for the Holy Spirit came to put the Spirit of Jesus within the disciples. Jesus said he would go away but that he would come again to them – in the power and presence of the Spirit. And the coming of the Spirit has put God and Christ in the most vital place – within.

For reading & meditation – Acts 2:1-21

Sub-Christian living

For this God ... will be our guide even to the end.
Psalm 48:14

God wants to guide us not only in times of emergency but at all times. One of the blessings of having the Holy Spirit within is that we gain the sense of being led. And not just the *sense* of being led but the practical benefits that come from it. God being who he is – the Architect of fine detail – he must have a plan, a purpose for every life. If we turn our backs on that idea then we are at a level that is sub-Christian.

For reading & meditation – Psalm 48:1-14

Continuous guidance

We are therefore Christ's ambassadors ...
2 Corinthians 5:20

Each life has peculiar significance. If we find that plan of God for us and work within it, we cannot fail. Outside of that plan we cannot succeed. To be the instrument of the purposes of God is the highest thing in life. "You did not choose me, but I chose you and appointed you to go and bear fruit" (John 15:16). Everyone must feel a sense of being a representative. We are speaking, thinking, acting in a Name that is not our own. That is why guidance is not a matter of the occasional but the continuous.

For reading & meditation – 2 Corinthians 5:11-21

Guidance demands surrender

He guides the humble in what is right and teaches them his way.
Psalm 25:9

The whole thought of guidance, whether it is occasional or continuous, strikes at the citadel of the personality and demands the surrender of self-sufficiency. If we are to be guided then there must be a shifting from self-will to God's will. That will, not your own, becomes supreme. God's will becomes your constant frame of reference. Guidance is the very essence of Christianity. It gives mission to life. But the mission demands submission.

For reading & meditation – Psalm 25:1-22

Healthy dependency

... should not a people enquire of their God?
Isaiah 8:19

It's surprising how many Christians there are who, though they know God, know little about his guidance, either occasional or continuous. The Spirit guides us in a way that does not override our personality or weaken it, but brings us to a point of healthy dependency. Some would say that dependency on another is unhealthy. Deeply entrenched in all of us is a spirit of independence and one of the biggest struggles we have as Christians is to bring our sinful and stubborn natures into submission to the divine will. Our need to be guided is often greater than our willingness.

For reading & meditation – Isaiah 8:11-22

Five forms of guidance

The Spirit told Phillip, "Go to that chariot and stay near it."
Acts 8:29

These are the general routes to guidance: first, guidance according to the character of Christ. We know who God wants us to be like – he wants us to be like his Son. Second, guidance through his Word. Third, guidance through circumstances – putting us in situations where the circumstances indicate the direction in which we ought to go. Fourth, guidance through the counsel of good and godly people. Fifth, guidance through the direct whispering of the Spirit within us. This last form of guidance is the direct voice of the Spirit in our hearts.

For reading & meditation – Acts 8:26-40

Listen!

Then Samuel said, "Speak, for your servant is listening."
1 Samuel 3:10

There are two main reasons why people fail to hear the Spirit's voice: their spiritual ears are untrained or they are unwilling. Many of us don't want to listen to the voice of God because we are afraid that if God reveals his will to us, it will be disagreeable. When you commune with God, give as much time to listening as you do to talking. At first you will not be able to distinguish the voice of the subconscious from the voice of the Spirit, but in time the differentiation will be possible. Sometimes, of course, the Spirit booms so loudly in the soul that his voice is unmistakable.

For reading & meditation – 1 Samuel 3:1-21

The great Teacher

"You are Israel's teacher," said Jesus,
"and do you not understand these things?"
John 3:10

Non-directive counselling helps people clarify their own thinking concerning their problems and then come to their own conclusions. However, true Christian counselling is at times non-directive, and at other times directive. Individuals who are struggling with a problem need clear direction on how to avail themselves of Christ's resources. Our Lord provides the supreme example of what and how to teach. No one can hold a candle to Christ's ministry – either in the Old Testament or in the New. He is seen in the Gospels teaching huge crowds, then at other times small groups.

For reading & meditation – John 3:1-15

Our Lord's "authority"

... he taught as one who had authority, and not as their teachers of the law.
Matthew 7:29

Obviously it was the "authority" with which Jesus spoke that arrested people's attention. Other teachers *quoted* authorities, but Jesus spoke *with* authority. What was that authority? It was the authority of the facts. He was uncovering Reality – Reality with a capital "R". He was the Revealer of the nature of Reality. He revealed first the nature and character of God, and went on to show how the nature and character of God is the ground of God's conduct and ours.

For reading & meditation – Matthew 7:15-28

The Spirit – our Teacher

... his anointing teaches you about all things ...
1 John 2:27

In the Person and teaching of Christ we have God's full and complete disclosure. The revelation which God has given us through Christ is final in the sense that nothing will be taught that is different from it, but we must see that it is also progressive and unfolding. In what respect? In the way that the Holy Spirit brings out from the words and teaching of Christ new understanding, new challenges and new insights. The divine Counsellor will teach us *all* Jesus taught but not *other* than Jesus taught.

For reading & meditation – 1 John 2:18-27

Lopsided Christianity

But when he, the Spirit of truth, comes,
he will guide you into all truth.
John 16:13

When we are not under the Holy Spirit's guidance, we can soon become focused on *some* thing that Jesus taught and neglect the "all". Whole denominations are built around one truth. This is not to say they don't believe other aspects of Christian teaching, but the truth they are always emphasising appears to make other truths less important by comparison. They live on a truth instead of on *the* Truth. Thus they have to be controversial to justify their lopsidedness. Christians who are truly open to the movement of the Holy Spirit in their lives will be creative rather than controversial.

For reading & meditation – John 16:5-16

Go the second mile

When the Counsellor comes ...
he will testify about me.
John 15:26

The Holy Spirit is not only our divine Teacher but also our divine Remembrancer. He promises to bring back to our remembrance all that Jesus said. What does this mean? It does not mean that the Holy Spirit will magically bring into our minds the words of Jesus if we have not taken the time to read them and ponder them. The more we expose ourselves to his words, the more easily the Spirit can remind us of them.

For reading & meditation – John 15:18-27

JUNE 15

Truth hurts

But when he, the Spirit of truth, comes,
he will guide you into all truth.
John 16:13

Counsellors are taught never to present an insight to someone without checking that the person understands what is being said and making sure they are following them every step of the way. Counsellors know too that if they present to someone a truth that is challenging or demanding, the personality more often than not becomes adept at looking for ways of escape. Thus skill is needed not only to present the truth but to outmanoeuvre the objections, overcome the difficulties, gently rebut the arguments, and thus guide people into possession of the truth. The Holy Spirit is expert not only in teaching truth but in guiding us into it.

For reading & meditation – John 16:5-16

JUNE 16

The Spirit of truth

... we speak, not in words taught us by human wisdom but in words taught by the Spirit ...
1 Corinthians 2:13

Think about times in your past when the Holy Spirit has guided you or disclosed something to you that put the truth about a matter into clear perspective. Can't that be understood as the Spirit guiding you into all truth? Can the promise of being guided into truth be seen also in the way the Spirit opens up a difficult scripture, or the truth regarding both options in a difficult decision? Why can't these be part of the truth which Jesus promised would be disclosed to you and me? Our Lord was an expert Teacher. And so is the Holy Spirit also.

For reading & meditation – 1 Corinthians 2:10-16 and Galatians 1:11-12

"Being there"

After six days Jesus took with him Peter, James and John the brother of James ...
Matthew 17:1

When the disciples discovered their Master was going to a cross, they drew back in dismay. The six days of confusion would be ended by the act of Transfiguration, but what must it have been like for our Lord and his disciples as they walked together through the northern part of Israel? He, no doubt, was pained by their failure to understand, and they were pained by the revelation that their concept of Messiahship did not appear to match his. But he stayed with them. He was there for them even when they were not there for him.

For reading & meditation – Matthew 16:21-28; 17:1-11

Non-verbal but empowering

I have heard many things like these;
miserable comforters are you all!
Job 16:2

Being there is not giving advice; it is saying in non-verbal ways: "This is not the time for talking but, as far as I am able, I want to bear the pain with you." A man, whose wife ill-treated him and humiliated him in front of friends said the following: "My only wish is that I might be able through a Christlike attitude to give her a taste of how much God loves her, and, above all else, my longing is to be there for her until she leaves this world for eternity." A person could almost put those same words on the lips of the Holy Spirit.

For reading & meditation – Job 16:1-22

Counsellor and Comforter

As a mother comforts her child,
so will I comfort you ...
Isaiah 66:13

Let's face it, some of the problems we encounter are not going to go away no matter how hard we pray. So what sort of help can we expect to receive from our divine Counsellor? The Greek term for the Holy Spirit is *parakletos*, derived from *para* (beside) and *kaleo* (call), and means "one who comes alongside to help". "Counsellor and Comforter" is a phrase which would convey the fuller idea that the Holy Spirit is not just someone who gives us advice but someone who feels *for* us and *with* us also.

For reading & meditation – Isaiah 66:5-13

The ultimate Counsellor

But God, who comforts the downcast,
comforted us by the coming of Titus ...
2 Corinthians 7:6

The Holy Spirit is a Counsellor who does more than give us advice; he enters into our hurts, empathises with our pain, and is there for us in every difficult situation of life. The word comforter – con (with) and fortis (strength) – means one who strengthens you by being with you. It's astonishing what strength we draw from someone just being with us when we are going through a painful experience. Simply sensing he is at our side is a comfort that we can never explain.

For reading & meditation – 2 Corinthians 7:1-16

The Spirit's first work

... Repent and be baptised ... And you will receive the gift of the Holy Spirit.
Acts 2:38

There are those who claim that the *first* task of the Holy Spirit is not really a work at all. Primarily, they say, he is there to be with us. What he does in us and through us is important, but his primary service is *to be there for us*. Many Christians seem to be more taken up with possessing the gifts of the Spirit than possessing the Holy Spirit himself. Peter talks about the Holy Spirit being *the* gift. He is the gift of gifts, and when he is with us and in us then he supplies us with the gifts that enhance our spiritual effectiveness.

For reading & meditation – Acts 2:29-41

"Trust my love"

My ears had heard of you but
now my eyes have seen you.
Job 42:5

There are occasions in life when problems don't go away despite our most ardent praying. At such times the divine Counsellor ministers to us his comfort and supernatural strength. There are many times in a person's life when the Holy Spirit whispers in his soul: "I cannot shield you from this. You will have to go through it, and you may feel some pain. But I will be with you all the way." Job never got the answers he wanted to his questions, but he received something better: he came through his experiences with a richer sense of God's presence than he had ever felt before.

For reading & meditation – Job 42:1-17

Supernatural comfort

... the church ... was strengthened; and encouraged by the Holy Spirit, it grew in numbers ...
Acts 9:31

The comforting ministry of the Holy Spirit is not simply a theory; it is a glorious fact. Who, reading these lines, has not felt the divine Counsellor's consoling presence steal into their souls during a time of personal difficulty or distress? The Holy Spirit's work is to bestow not human comfort but *supernatural* comfort. I must do my part and trust him to do his. All who belong to Christ's Body are expected to minister comfort to each other, but the biggest share belongs to the Holy Spirit. We comfort; he is the Comforter.

For reading & meditation – Acts 9:19b-31

Grace – simply amazing

Three times I pleaded with the Lord to take it away from me.
2 Corinthians 12:8

Paul doesn't tell us what his problem was but uses a metaphor – a thorn in the flesh – which is used elsewhere in Scripture to convey a troublesome issue. Paul asked the Lord three times to take it away but the answer was "No". But in the midst of his trouble God began to pour into Paul a special supply of his comforting grace; grace to accept the "No", grace to endure the discomfort and grace to handle the pain. But how does grace work? As you pray the heaviness in your spirit continues, but then suddenly, it is as if a weight is lifted from you. You breathe more easily and your spirit feels a little lighter.

For reading & meditation – 2 Corinthians 12:1-10

Brave if not blithe

Shout for joy, O heavens ... For the Lord comforts his people and will have compassion on his afflicted ones.
Isaiah 49:13

In a fallen universe like this we are confronted with issues which produce almost inconsolable pain. Why did God allow sin to strike the universe in such a way? Could he now have modified its consequences so it would not have affected us as it has? We will understand everything one day, but meanwhile God simply says: "Here's my comfort, you can get by with this." In moments of bewilderment it is not answers we need; it is comfort. That comfort may not keep us blithe but it will keep us brave.

For reading & meditation – Isaiah 49:8-16

When the world goes grey

... you, O Lord, have helped me and comforted me.
Psalm 86:17

Sooner or later every one of us needs comfort. It does not matter how strong we may be, how composed and free from sentimentality, the time will come when we need to feel God's solace. The Holy Spirit is the minister of grace. He is the One who brings into our hearts the resources of the Godhead. What about nature, or music, or art? They can be helpful supplements but they can never be substitutes. They are not a fount of comfort in themselves. The only sure comfort when all the world has gone grey is the comfort of God.

For reading & meditation – Psalm 86:1-17

Is optimism enough?

Is there no balm in Gilead?
Jeremiah 8:22

There are in the Christian Church those who advocate optimism as the way to approach life's problems. You sometimes see posters outside churches designed to catch people's attention with a cheerful word. But those who choose the words for some of these posters, as well as those who display them, seem to have no understanding of what is relevant to the needs of the general public. The only reality we can depend upon in the hard and cruel world is the consolation of the Holy Spirit. Many things may be absent. But God's comfort. Never.

For reading & meditation – Jeremiah 8:14-22

Wait till you get home

He will wipe every tear from their eyes.
Revelation 21:4

We are not always going to receive answers to the difficult questions that arise during our lifetime. Questions such as these: Why has God allowed this? What possible good can come from it? How can a loving God permit such a thing? A good deal of frustration can be avoided if we settle for the fact that God knows what he is doing and that one day, not now but when we get to heaven, all will be made clear. The answers you don't get here, you will get in eternity. Here, however, you are guaranteed the strength you need to carry on.

For reading & meditation – Revelation 20:11-15; 21:1-5

What happens now?

Come near to God and he will come near to you.
James 4:8

As we make our way towards heaven life may be hard and perplexing, but God has given us his Holy Spirit to be our Counsellor along the way. How sad that with all the resources of our divine Counsellor available to us we prefer so often to muddle through on our own. When we refuse to open up to him, to depend on him and consult him, we deprive ourselves of the love, wisdom, and spiritual sustenance we need to live effectively and dynamically. He will open up to you, but only if you will open up to him. Take one step towards him and he will take two towards you.

For reading & meditation – James 4:1-17

JULY

What's in a name?

The words of Jeremiah son of Hilkiah ...
Jeremiah 1:1

Jeremiah's ministry is reflected in his name; it means the Lord hurls. Nowhere does Scripture reveal more clearly the meaning of spiritual faithfulness than in the life of Jeremiah. He kept true to the Word of God despite all the setbacks and struggles he was called to endure. There were times when the fiery darts of doubt pierced his heart but they were always quenched when, through open and honest prayer, he allowed God's presence to flow into his soul. The greatest thing anyone can do in this life is to fulfil their spiritual destiny. Jeremiah shows us *how*.

For reading & meditation – Jeremiah 1:1-3

The larger story

Before I formed you in the womb I knew you ...
Jeremiah 1:5

"Before I formed you in the womb," says the Almighty, "*I knew you.*" This statement is intended to help Jeremiah understand that he is part of a larger story. This first word of God to Jeremiah gives the prophet a centre of gravity not in himself or his circumstances but in his Creator. Jeremiah was a prescription baby – made for the task which God had foreseen he could best accomplish. And so are you. You too have been chosen for something important that God is doing in this generation. It is something that nobody other than you can do.

For reading & meditation – Jeremiah 1:4-5

Not my ability but his

Then the Lord ... said to me, "Now, I have put my words in your mouth."
Jeremiah 1:9

The Bible is full of examples of people who, whenever they were asked by God to do something special for him, started pleading their inadequacy. Each person is utterly inadequate for the tasks God asks us to do for him. It is not wrong to feel inadequate. But we must be careful not to let those feelings lead us to despair. Rather they should lead us to a deeper dependency on the Lord. "God does not send us into the dangerous and exacting life of faith because we are qualified, he chooses us in order to qualify us for what he wants us to be and do."

For reading & meditation – Jeremiah 1:6-10

Shaped by a vision

Today I have made you a fortified city,
an iron pillar and a bronze wall ...
Jeremiah 1:18

How did Jeremiah change from lacking confidence to being secure in God? It came about through two remarkable visions. These two visions, the blossoming almond branch and the pot of boiling water have been described as "Jeremiah's Oxford and Cambridge" – in other words, his core curriculum. He was being taught that he must never under-estimate God and never over-estimate evil. God never goes back on his Word and evil cannot triumph in the end. Only when we are shaped by that vision will we have the strength and courage to pursue the path that God has planned for us.

For reading & meditation – Jeremiah 1:11-19

How problems develop

My people have ... forsaken me ...
and have dug their own cisterns ...
Jeremiah 2:13

Jeremiah speaking on behalf of the Almighty, issues a powerful indictment against the people of Israel accusing them of spiritual promiscuity. He sums up their spiritual condition. It consists of two great sins: first, forsaking the spring of living water and second, digging their own water-storage cisterns. People refuse to slake their thirst in God, preferring instead to find stagnant water in a "cistern" of their own making – money, power, status, and so on. This attitude of independence is the energy which makes many of our emotional and psychological problems grow.

For reading & meditation – Jeremiah 2:1-18

Shocking language

You are a swift she-camel running here and there ...
Jeremiah 2:23

When addressing the Christians in Laodicea, our Lord threatened to "spit you out of my mouth" (Rev. 3:16). Why does he use such uncharacteristic, even shocking language? Because complacent people *need* to be shocked. Perhaps this is why the Almighty chooses these vivid and unflattering word pictures to describe the condition into which Judah had fallen. When God's people desire the things that lie outside of God's will so much so that they will do anything to get it, then it is a sure sign of a dire spiritual condition that needs to be sternly confronted.

For reading & meditation – Jeremiah 2:19-32

Sin breaks God's heart

"Return, faithless Israel," declares the Lord, "I will frown on you no longer ..."
Jeremiah 3:12

Jeremiah reminds Israel of the law given to Moses that forbade a divorced couple to be reunited to each other (v.1; Deut. 24:1-4). The purpose of this law was to maintain a high view of marriage and to protect relationships from being degraded to the casual level in which a man could divorce his wife and have her back whenever he felt like it. A society that has a low view of marriage is inevitably defiled. God turns from upbraiding and shocking them to wooing them. "Return ... and I will cure you of backsliding". The most awful thing about sin is not simply that it breaks God's laws, but that it breaks his heart.

For reading & meditation – Jeremiah 3:1-25

The first move is ours

... the Lord says ... "Break up your unploughed ground and do not sow among thorns ..."
Jeremiah 4:3

We always need to keep in mind that whenever we move away from our relationship with God either through a sin of commission or a sin of ommission, *the only way back is the way of repentance.* Repentance is not merely being sorry about sin, but being sorry enough to quit. Jeremiah reminded the people that they needed to remove the sin that hardened their heart before the good seed of God's Word could take root. If we say to God, "Restore me and then I will give up my sin," the result is a spiritual stalemate. The first move must be ours.

For reading & meditation – Jeremiah 4:1-4

Are you listening?

Hear this, you ... have eyes but do not see ... ears but do not hear ...
Jeremiah 5:21

There is a saying that "there are none so deaf as those who do not wish to hear, none so blind as those who do not wish to see." Our Lord made the same criticism of some of the people of his day: "You will be ever hearing but never understanding; you will be ever seeing but never perceiving" (Matt. 13:14). Nothing can be more spiritually damaging than to tune God out when he is speaking. Those who think that the problem in their spiritual life is that God doesn't speak to them may find that the problem is rather that they are not listening to a God who is always trying to speak.

For reading & meditation – Jeremiah 5:18-31

Healing wounds "lightly"

They dress the wound of my people
as though it were not serious ...
Jeremiah 6:14

People who are called by God to apply spiritual remedies to serious matters do so in a way that only heals the wound "lightly". Ministers, leaders, counsellors and others who offer spiritual direction do the people of God a disservice when they deal only with symptoms instead of confronting, for example, the issues of sin in a person's life when sin is the root of their problem. Christians who treat the issue of sin lightly deserve no recognition as spiritual leaders.

For reading & meditation – Jeremiah 6:1-15

The past is important

Stand at the crossroads and look;
ask for the ancient paths ...
Jeremiah 6:16

There is a crisis of confidence amongst many in relation to the ancient Scriptures and some are asking whether the Bible is as relevant in modern times as it was in the past. When we talk about truth and morality we are not dealing with Victorian, Edwardian, or even the modern Elizabethan values. We are dealing with the living and timeless God. To live successfully in the present and the future we must listen to the past. There *are* ancient paths marked out for us by God. To stray from them is to put our lives in peril.

For reading & meditation – Jeremiah 6:16-30

Deceptive words

But look, you are trusting in deceptive words that are worthless.
Jeremiah 7:8

We need to be careful that our words match our behaviour. Though Christians may not *say* lies in church, they often *sing* them. Take for example these lines: "I surrender all". "Take my silver and my gold." "I will follow where he leadeth." Do we really mean what we sing? Or do we fool ourselves into thinking that the more religious phrases we use the safer we are spiritually? "Standing in a church singing a hymn doesn't make us holy any more than standing in a barn and neighing makes us a horse." It's not so much what we say but who we are that's important.

For reading & meditation – Jeremiah 7:1-11

"*I am sorry!*"

When men fall down, do they not get up?
Jeremiah 8:4

In the moral realm we don't like admitting that we have erred. Out of a long list of statements which people found difficult to say, the one they found *most* difficult was: "I am sorry." If we remain perverse and unrepentant then judgment has to be meted out. God's judgment on our sinfulness may seem harsh and hard but it is prompted more by love than indignation. He loves us as we are, but *he* loves us too much to let us stay as we are. The first step to moving in the right direction begins with the words "*I am sorry.*"

For reading & meditation – Jeremiah 8:1-21

When did you last weep?

Oh, that my head were a spring of water
and my eyes a fountain of tears!
Jeremiah 9:1

How do we feel about the pitiable state of the Church and the world? Does it drive us to our knees in fervent intercessory prayer? When did we last weep over the condition of both the world and the Church? However ashamed we feel we must not leave it there. We must ask God to forgive our lack of compassion and invite him to break our hearts for the world he so deeply loves. Godly concern is not something that can be manufactured. It comes only as we are willing to press our hearts against his. And it is the source of true prayer.

For reading & meditation – Jeremiah 9:1-26

We must worship

No-one is like you, O Lord ...
Jeremiah 10:6

Worship makes it possible for God to enter our lives and to be to us all that he promises to be. But we cannot truly worship God without at the same time obeying him. An idol helps us express our need to worship without the necessity for inward change. That is why idolatry is so appealing. We can express our need to worship without having to make those deep inward changes which the true God demands. Those who do not worship the true God will worship something else, for they *must* worship.

For reading & meditation – Jeremiah 10:1-16

Unfaithful in marriage

Both the house of Israel and the house of Judah have broken the covenant I made with their forefathers.
Jeremiah 11:10

The Almighty refers to his people as his "beloved" (v. 15); with the marital relationship in mind he condemns them for spiritual adultery. A time comes when God must inevitably judge sinful behaviour. There is no point in asking God to bless our lives when we are engaged in wilful sin. His demands are not unreasonable. Thankfully he does not wipe us out every time we err. He is incredibly patient with our frailties. But he cannot tolerate repeated rebellious sin. The judgements of God are not unreasonable but they are inevitable.

For reading & meditation – Jeremiah 11:1-17

Dealing with doubts

You are always righteous, O Lord,
when I bring a case before you.
Jeremiah 12:1

Jeremiah was told by God that people were planning to kill him. Jeremiah changes from being a confident prophet to a man seemingly plagued with doubts. Is he guilty of leading a double life? Was he a hero when standing before a crowd, but a coward in private? His reaction is that of any normal person in such circumstances. There is nothing wrong in having doubts; it is what we do with those doubts which is important. Doubt is best dealt with in prayer before God, not peddled in public.

For reading & meditation – Jeremiah 11:18-12:4

Struggling well

Yet I would speak with you about your justice:
Why does the way of the wicked prosper?
Jeremiah 12:1

The realistic Christian says, "I am discouraged and I will bring it to God in heartfelt prayer." The unrealistic Christian says "God is on the throne, and because of that I can never be discouraged." Being honest with one's feelings is a mark of maturity, not of immaturity. Jeremiah's struggles continued for most of his life, but he learned to struggle well. That means relying not on our own strength of character but on the strength of God's righteous character, whose justice is real even if it is not always obvious as we struggle against the situations which discourage us.

For reading & meditation – Jeremiah 12:1-4

Running with horses

If you have raced with men on foot and they have worn you out, how can you compete with horses?
Jeremiah 12:5

The Almighty is not in the business of explaining things but in getting us to trust him. Jeremiah was in danger of lapsing into self-pity and the remedy is not a doctrinal statement but a challenge. God gives him a bracing reply: *If you raced with men on foot and they have worn you out how can you compete with horses?* If Jeremiah can't trust God in the darkness how will he trust him in a raging storm? He responded not by argument but by action. He rose to the challenge. He *ran with the horses.*

For reading & meditation – Jeremiah 12:1-17

Curious but not convicted

For as a belt is bound round a man's waist, so I bound the whole house of ... Judah to me ...
Jeremiah 13:11

Jeremiah used the picture of winejars. He is commanded to tell the people: "Every wineskin should be filled with wine," a popular saying of the day. When they gave the usual response, "I agree," Jeremiah was to tell them: "That's not what I mean ... everyone living in this land will be filled with helpless bewilderment." Unless you act on what God is saying one day you will stagger like drunken men spiritually and socially lost and confused. Such words and actions aroused the people's curiosity, but did nothing to change their minds. Persistent sin can so dull our conscience that no matter what God does we cannot hear him.

For reading & meditation – Jeremiah 13:1-14

God – an unhurried judge

Can the Ethiopian change his skin or the leopard its spots?
Jeremiah 13:23

Evil had so gripped the people that it was now a lifestyle they could not change anymore than an Ethiopian could change the colour of his skin or a leopard its spots. Why were so many warnings given and why did God take so long to pour out judgment? He does not want anyone to perish but wants all to come to repentance (2 Peter 3:9). God's unhurried ways might encourage us to think casually about his inevitable judgement on sin. If we do, then we think wrongly. Praise him for his patience which waited for you, but don't try his patience with persistent sin.

For reading & meditation – Jeremiah 13:15-27

God has feelings too

... Let my eyes overflow with tears night and day without ceasing; for ... my people ... has suffered a grievous wound, a crushing blow.
Jeremiah 14:17

Jeremiah is told to stop praying as God's mind is already made up. Jeremiah is to be commended for his desire to intercede for his people but he is out of touch with their stubborn commitment to independence. How does God feel about all this? Never forget – God has feelings too. It breaks his heart to see the waywardness and obstinacy of his people. How different our lives would be if we could see that sin is not just a collision with the divine will but a wound in the divine heart.

For reading & meditation – Jeremiah 14:1-21

Spiritual stalemate

Even if Moses and Samuel were to stand before me, my heart would not go out to this people.
Jeremiah 15:1

Intercession is a vital part of the Christian life but what should one do when God says "Stop praying?" When Moses and Samuel prayed, the people displayed a readiness to repent. The nation at the time of Jeremiah, however, was stubborn, obstinate and recalcitrant. Jeremiah's intercessions, though sincere and well meaning, did not reflect the true mood of the people. They wanted God to do his part, but they were not prepared to do theirs. Hence, they were locked in spiritual stalemate and could not move forward with God. God's blessings are there to be taken, but they are never to be taken for granted.

For reading & meditation – Jeremiah 14:22 & 15:1-4

"My wound is grievous"

Why is my pain unending and my wound grievous and incurable?
Jeremiah 15:18

All Jeremiah's fear, loneliness, hurt and anger are poured out into God's ear. Some people think of prayer as a time of quiet and calm solitude before God, but it can be a time of great personal struggle also. God will never be against us for honest praying. In God's presence we need pretend about nothing, because God sees and knows us as we really are. And he understands our feelings of hurt and anger; it is not sinful to feel such things, although they may lead us to sin if we don't share them with God.

For reading & meditation – Jeremiah 15:1-18

JULY 24

Renewed and restored

If you repent, I will restore you ...
Jeremiah 15:19

Whenever we sin there is *only* one way back to God. And that is through the door of repentance. Admit your misplaced dependency, God is saying. If you repent of it you will be restored. You will stand on your feet once again. God doesn't change, neither does his Word change. But we do. And when doubt and fear cause us temporarily to lose our bearings, if we are willing to admit it and repent of it then God delights to restore us and confirm afresh the work to which he has called us.

For reading & meditation – Jeremiah 15:19-21

Whose side are you on?

Let this people turn to you, but
you must not turn to them.
Jeremiah 15:19

Christians involved in pastoral ministry can easily find themselves taking the side of the people against God, rather than standing solidly on the side of the Almighty. This is not to say that we must lose our compassion for people, or fail in our responsibility to intercede for them. But where obstinacy and rebellion remain in the heart, no matter what the extenuating circumstances, sin must be identified and God's perspective made clear. When it comes to a matter of sin there is only one side – God's side.

For reading & meditation – Jeremiah 15:19-21

No private life

You must not marry and have
sons or daughters in this place.
Jeremiah 16:2

Jeremiah's personal life was to be an object lesson, an acted parable, about Judah's condition. Compared to the serious spiritual condition into which Israel had fallen, and the devastation that was to come upon them because of that, *the loneliness which came from being without a wife and family was as nothing*. There is no such thing as a private life for those who commit their ways to God. Our time, money and relationships all belong to him. A measure of the depth of our spiritual commitment would be to ask ourselves: what would I not give up if required by God to do so?

For reading & meditation – Jeremiah 16:1-12

Keeping Sunday special

... keep the Sabbath day holy, as
I commanded your forefathers.
Jeremiah 17:22

Sabbath keeping had always been taken as a sign of loyalty to God ever since it was laid down at Sinai. Those who sought to keep it showed signs of spiritual health; those who profaned it showed signs of spiritual ill-health. The Sabbath was usually the first thing to be violated when the people began to backslide. We should see it as a gift from God that gives us more freedom than usual to focus on him, worship him, and to enjoy fellowship with others who also love and serve him. Whatever the world thinks of the Sabbath the Church should think of it as special.

For reading & meditation – Jeremiah 17:19-27

The potter's house

... so the potter formed it into another pot, shaping it as seemed best to him.
Jeremiah 18:4

Though we mess up God's original purposes for our lives by our recalcitrancy and stubbornness, he nevertheless pursues his purposes with us still. It might not be what he originally wanted. But his skill and power can make something of us beyond what we dare imagine or even deserve. If by your sin or failure you have frustrated God's original purpose but have repented and come back to God, take heart. He may not be able to achieve his original purpose but he can make something beautiful of you still.

For reading & meditation – Jeremiah 18:1-12

A ministers' conference

... I will smash this nation and this city
just as this potter's jar is smashed ...
Jeremiah 19:11

Whereas a spoiled vessel on a potter's wheel could be reshaped, once it had hardened it was beyond reshaping and was fit only for breaking. Many a modern-day ministers' conference could do with a visit from Jeremiah, especially where leaders have lost their confidence in the Scriptures and close their eyes to waywardness and sin. And many a church might profit from a few jugs being broken in the middle of a service to bring home to the congregation the inevitable consequences of sin.

For reading & meditation – Jeremiah 19:1-15

What screams the loudest?

Sing to the Lord! Give praise to the Lord!
Jeremiah 20:13

Jeremiah accuses God of deceiving him, of failing him and of bullying him. Jeremiah had allowed God's Word to penetrate his being to such an extent that in the moment of overwhelming test it was the divine Word that cried out the loudest. If we allow God's Word to so live and take root within us, when our hurts and frustrations scream within God's Word will burn in us with his warming love, and we will hear his message above the din.

For reading & meditation – Jeremiah 20:1-13

AUGUST

Swinging emotions

Why did I ever come out of the womb to see trouble and sorrow ...
Jeremiah 20:18

Faith and doubt are locked together within Jeremiah and he finds it difficult to endure the strain of the tension. How can he at one and the same time claim that God is within like a mighty warrior (v. 11) and then in the next breath curse the day he was born (v. 14)? And why did he write it down? Those who have battled with discouragement and despair will understand. Jesus would have understood. Whatever is going on must not be denied. Tell God honestly how you feel. In his presence no anguish need be stifled or repressed.

For reading & meditation – Jeremiah 20:14-18

The new shoot

The days are coming ... when I will raise up ... a righteous Branch ...
Jeremiah 23:5

The name given to the future Saviour indicates his true character – *the Lord Our Righteousness*. The "shoot" that will emerge – our Lord Jesus Christ – will impart to people a righteousness, which is not earned by works but given through grace. The high ideals commanded at Sinai which people felt were utterly beyond them will at last become realisable through a new covenant sealed in Christ's blood. Our Lord not only imputes righteousness to our spiritual account, he also imparts it to our daily lives.

For reading & meditation – Jeremiah 23:1-8

False prophets

... My heart is broken within me ... because of the Lord and his holy words.
Jeremiah 23:9

A false prophet may appear to live according to God's design but in fact he does not. He tampers with God's message, puts a spin on it, and makes it more palatable. He encourages his listeners (usually subtly) to risk displeasing God, he tends to be arrogant, self-serving and more interested in pleasing people than in pleasing God. There are more false prophets in the church of today than we might imagine. Thankfully God has given us the Bible – *a more sure word of prophecy* – by which to test all other prophecies and teachings.

For reading & meditation – Jeremiah 23:9-40

Thank God for trouble

The good (figs) are very good, but the poor ones ... cannot be eaten.
Jeremiah 24:3

The future lay not with those who had been carried into captivity in Babylon. The exiles would be so shocked by their change of circumstances that their hearts would respond readily to God's Word, whereas those who remained in Jerusalem would continue to be stubborn and obstinate. It's a sad fact that sometimes God has to corner us before we admit that his way is best. Trouble is often a blessing in disguise. Where would you and I be now if God had not loved us enough to chastise us at certain periods in our lives? We would be like bad figs, fit only to be thrown out.

For reading & meditation – Jeremiah 24:1-10

Twenty-three years!

For twenty-three years ... the word of the Lord has come to me and I have spoken to you ...
Jeremiah 25:3

Jeremiah lived for God the only way – one day at a time. The pursuit of excellence requires the ability and commitment to keep returning to the task you know God has called you to and never to give up. It might sound dull and boring doing the same thing day after day but if God has commanded it, it is never the *same* thing. Nothing can be greater than to do whatever God wants us to do. We will never be bored by it.

For reading & meditation – Jeremiah 25:1-14

Never give up!

... the Lord ... said to me: "Take from my hand this cup ..."
Jeremiah 25:15

You have been labouring faithfully at the task for many years, but there don't seem to be many positive results. Life is hard for you and nobody seems to appreciate you. If Jeremiah was there with you he would probably say, "I know how you feel." When God gives us a task he wants us to stick to it no matter what happens. Perseverance is not a popular idea today. But it is one which carries great weight in heaven. God never gives out impossible or fruitless tasks, and he never gives up on us.

For reading & meditation – Jeremiah 25:15-38

Thank God for the laity

... I will make this house like Shiloh
and this city an object of cursing ...
Jeremiah 26:6

We should be deeply thankful for the ministry of what is sometimes referred to as the laity: the body of men and women who though untrained at a seminary level delve deeply into the Word of God and are experienced in applying it to their lives in the world. Without such people we would lose a perspective on the Scriptures which the best Bible College in the world may be unable to convey to trainee ministers.

For reading & meditation – Jeremiah 26:1-24

Under God's yoke

... Bow your neck under the yoke
of the king of Babylon ...
Jeremiah 27:12

Nebuchadnezzar was one of the most ruthless, despotic, and godless men who has ever walked the face of the earth. How could he be described as God's "servant"? Without realising it, Nebuchadnezzar was being used to advance the purposes of the Almighty, even though he was a worshipper of idols. God is not limited to working through his own people. He has the whole world and its peoples in his hand. They are under his yoke. We may find events mysterious, and wonder what God is doing. Jeremiah reminds us that God is doing something, even if we don't understand it.

For reading & meditation – Jeremiah 27:1-22

Prophet against prophet

At this, the prophet Jeremiah went on his way.
Jeremiah 28:11

It is sad when people prefer to listen to comforting lies rather than to the painful truth. How different life would be for many of us if we were secure enough in God to walk away from unnecessary arguments instead of bandying words to no avail. Jeremiah was not afraid of an argument but he was not drawn into one simply for the sake of it, *even though he knew that he was right*! He felt no need to defend himself; he was content to let time tell who spoke truly. It's an example we should follow.

For reading & meditation – Jeremiah 28:1-17

Dear exiles, I love you

This is what the Lord Almighty .. says to all those I carried into exile ...
Jeremiah 29:4

Jeremiah knows that the exile had put the people in a position where their inner emptiness could be exposed, and now was the time for them to seek the Lord (v. 13). They hadn't done so when they were in freedom; perhaps now they were in captivity things would be different. Notice how tenderly he deals with the exiles. He doesn't say, "Serves you right! Stew there for a while!" He reassures them of his good plans and that one day he will restore them (vv. 11, 14). Sometimes God has to upset us in order to set us up.

For reading & meditation – Jeremiah 29:1-32

A book of hope

... you will be my people, and I will be your God.
Jeremiah 30:22

The prophecies Jeremiah makes have been compared to a range of mountain peaks. From a distance they look as if they are close to one another but actually they are great distances apart. He talks of events as if they will all happen together, but in fact there will be enormous time differences between them. He sees the end of the exile but he also sees the day when Christ will come as King and reign for ever. *You will be my people and I will be your God.* It applies as much to you and me as it did to Jeremiah's listeners.

For reading & meditation – Jeremiah 30:1-24

AUGUST 11

Invest in the future

Jeremiah said, "The word of the Lord came to me ..."
Jeremiah 32:6

It's one thing to say you have faith and confidence that God will bring about what he has promised; it's another thing to put that faith into operation. We call it "putting your money where your mouth is." God may delay his promises but he will never deny them. Perhaps to act with confidence is the very step of faith God is wanting you to take.

For reading & meditation – Jeremiah 32:1-15

God is merciful

Ah, Sovereign Lord ... Nothing is too hard for you.
Jeremiah 32:17

When Jeremiah prays he concentrates on God's great redemptive acts (vv. 20-22). He concludes by referring to the sins and failing of the past (v. 23), the difficulties being experienced in the present (v. 24), and the mystery of the future (v. 25). How does God respond to such a prayer? He announces that though judgment is at hand his last word is not judgment, but mercy. God has to judge. He cannot do any other and still remain God. The delight of his heart, however, is to restore, to forgive, and to pour out his blessings on his people.

For reading & meditation – Jeremiah 32:16-44

Turn your face to God

Call to me and I will answer you and tell you great and unsearchable things you do not know.
Jeremiah 33:3

Why is it that often when we need help, guidance, or encouragement, the last person we call upon is the Lord? "It ought to be the soul's habit whenever discouraged or in need of guidance to first call out to the Lord before calling out to anyone else." God can make himself heard and known of course without us calling on him. The whole of the Bible is evidence of that. But what he longs for is a relationship with us. Talk to a person's face rather than their back. God does too.

For reading & meditation – Jeremiah 33:1-26

Permanent or temporary?

Recently you repented ... But
now you have turned round ...
Jeremiah 34:15, 16

What do we do when we are in a tight spot? We panic and bargain with God, promising that if he delivers us we will be more faithful in prayer, reading the Scriptures and giving to his work. Then when the difficulty has passed we soon forget our promises and go back to living the way we did before. Nothing sharpens up our spiritual lives like a threat to our welfare. But when the threat is over we go right back to living the way we lived before. God looks for permanent heart-changes, not temporary mind-changes.

For reading & meditation – Jeremiah 34:1-21

Recabite resolve

Go to the Recabite family ... and
give them wine to drink!
Jeremiah 35:2

The Recabites were widely known for their refusal to drink alcohol. Why then would God, through Jeremiah, invite them to break their pledge and to drink wine? God knew that they would not yield to the temptation. He wanted to use this incident to show that here was a group of people committed to the word of a man who lived centuries ago, while Judah's people generally refused to commit themselves to the Word that God was speaking to them now. Is it possible that we, the present people of God, are more loyal to customs than the law of God? It can happen very easily, but we can see it only with difficulty.

For reading & meditation – Jeremiah 35:1-19

God can't be stopped

Take another scroll and write on it all the words that were on the first scroll ...
Jeremiah 36:28

Jeremiah appoints Baruch to read to the assembled people the words which had been recorded. When eventually the king hears the scroll being read, he takes a knife, cuts the scroll into pieces and throws it into the fire. This is the first record of the Word of God being destroyed. God responds by commanding Jeremiah to compile a new scroll. It is foolish to think anyone can outmanoeuvre God. He can turn every reverse into a forward direction. The Almighty is never stymied. Remember this incident next time you face opposition or setbacks.

For reading & meditation – Jeremiah 36:1-32

Who should change?

... King Zedekiah ... asked ... "Is there any word from the Lord?"
Jeremiah 37:17

King Zedekiah asks Jeremiah to pray that God will turn the situation around. But Jeremiah had already been told to stop praying against defeat (7:16; 14:11). It was a profitless exercise as God's mind was already made up. The prophet informs the king that the siege would be resumed eventually and that Jerusalem, as he had predicted many times, would fall into enemy hands. Zedekiah wanted God to change but he himself didn't want to change. This is typical of human nature. We plead for God to change his mind so that we will not have to change ours.

For reading & meditation – Jeremiah 37:1-21

Standing for justice

... these men have acted wickedly in all they have done to Jeremiah the prophet.
Jeremiah 38:9

Ebed-Melech feared God more than man. He alone among all the palace officials stood against the murder plot. It is noteworthy that because of this he was spared when Jerusalem fell (39:15-18). How many of us have the courage to speak up when we see injustice being done? All that needs to happen for evil to flourish is for good people to do nothing. Do we slink into the shadows or do we stand up for God and for right? It may increase antagonism towards us, but Jesus promised we will not lose our reward in heaven because we do such things for him (Matt. 25:34-40).

For reading & meditation – Jeremiah 38:1-13

Zedekiah, the marshmallow

King Zedekiah said ... "I am afraid of the Jews who have gone over to the Babylonians ..."
Jeremiah 38:19

Reputation is what other people think of you. Character is what you are in the depth of your being. Zedekiah had no stomach for facing reality. He wanted changes on the outside without being prepared to change on the inside. Zedekiah was soft like a marshmallow, and Jeremiah was firm like a rock. One pursued self-interest; the other pursued excellence. Every day we face a choice – living for ourselves and caving in to others' opinions or living for God and standing firm on his truth.

For reading & meditation – Jeremiah 38:14-28

The fall of Jerusalem

Take him and look after him; don't harm him but do for him whatever he asks.
Jeremiah 39:12

What a difference there is between the fates of Zedekiah and Jeremiah. One was saved by faith; the other was destroyed by fear. One was filled with self-interest, the other with compassion for his people. One was treated with contempt, the other with respect. A life of commitment to the Lord can sometimes be tough, but God often has special blessings or compensations for his faithful people. He allows us to be tempted, but he promises also to make a way of escape. He allows us to suffer, but he promises to support us and bring good out of evil.

For reading & meditation – Jeremiah 39:1-18

The choice

So Jeremiah ... stayed ... among the people who were left behind in the land.
Jeremiah 40:6

Jeremiah is being offered a chance to retire in Babylon. He was about sixty-five at the time so the offer had its attractions. If anyone deserved a life of ease with special facilities, it was Jeremiah. But the prophet was not ready for retirement. It didn't take him long to make up his mind. Jeremiah chose to return to Jerusalem and live as he had always lived, trusting God and confident in his purposes. Jeremiah's choice that day at Rama was typical of how he had lived all his life. He chose to be where the Almighty had enshrined his Name – Jerusalem, the city of God.

For reading & meditation – Jeremiah 40:1-16

Easy way or God's way?

They were afraid of them because Ishmael ... had killed Gedaliah ...
Jeremiah 41:18

Egypt represented safety and security – a much more appealing alternative than staying in Jerusalem, and depending on God to direct their lives. Jerusalem with its city reduced to rubble and its economy in ruins, was a hard option. Egypt was an easier one. Many of us, when faced with the choice between trusting the invisible God or putting our faith in the things we can see, prefer to do the equivalent of living in Egypt. Trusting God is not easy, especially where there is an escape route that leads to more tangible things. But they may prove unable to support us.

For reading & meditation – Jeremiah 41:1-18

Keep an open mind

I have told you today, but you still have
not obeyed the Lord your God ...
Jeremiah 42:21

We could be forgiven for thinking that Jeremiah's decision to return to Jerusalem meant that there, in the city of God, he would end his days. It was not to be. He ended his days in the place he had told his people not to go to – Egypt. God could not have put the issue more clearly – but Johanan spurned the advice given by the Lord and set off for Egypt, taking Jeremiah and his friend Baruch with him. We are not truly open to God; we don't take seriously the possibility that he might say "No"

For reading & meditation – Jeremiah 42:1-22

Egypt – no refuge

The Lord our God has not sent you to say, "You must not go to Egypt to settle there."
Jeremiah 43:2

When Johanan and his associates asked Jeremiah to pray for God's guidance they really wanted God's confirmation of their plans to go down to Egypt. This is a problem many of us face for if we are honest we are more interested in getting God's approval for our own plans than seeking him for his. Never make any plans unless you are willing to have God change them, and never pray unless you are willing to accept God's answer. The things or people we trust may seem strong, but if they are not chosen by God they will let us down. It's sad, but is so often true.

For reading & meditation – Jeremiah 43:1-13

Jeremiah's last sermon

This word came to Jeremiah concerning all the Jews living in Lower Egypt ...
Jeremiah 44:1

One of the great principles of the Christian life is the further we drift from God, the more confused our thinking becomes and the more likely we are to perpetuate our mistakes. When we forget a lesson we are in danger of making the mistake again that the lesson was meant to counter. The people of Judah forgot their former sins and thus found it easy to repeat them. Our past is a school of experience. We live foolishly, even dangerously, when we fail to let our past mistakes point us in the direction God wishes us to take now.

For reading & meditation – Jeremiah 44:1-30

A boost to Baruch

Should you then seek great things
for yourself? Seek them not.
Jeremiah 45:5

When we concentrate more on our own careers or our own future than on the purpose of God for our lives we become ego-centred rather than God-centred. That does not mean it is wrong to think and plan out a career. It means rather that unless God has first claim on our lives then we live superficially no matter how much money we make or how many possessions we own. True greatness in his kingdom is serving him and others before ourselves (Luke 22:26-27).

For reading & meditation – Jeremiah 45:1-5

A message to the nations

This is the word of the Lord that came to Jeremiah the prophet concerning the nations ...
Jeremiah 46:1

No one has a greater missionary heart than God. His primary intention in calling Israel into covenant with himself was *evangelistic*. He wanted to be a shop window through which other nations could look in and see the advantages and blessings that come from serving the true and living God. But as we well know, Israel failed to reflect the divine purposes. Our churches ought not to be cosy places to which we retreat but centres from which we draw inspiration to make both individual and corporate evangelistic forays into the world. Jesus' last words were not "come", but "go" (Matt. 28:19).

For reading & meditation – Jeremiah 46:1-10

AUGUST 28

A tale of two cities

Babylon's thick wall will be levelled ...
Jeremiah 51:58

Babylon, built on the site of the original tower of Babel, represents the kind of pride that struts before the Almighty and says: "We can get along without you." Jerusalem, on the other hand, represents God-centred worship that says, "We can't get along without you." Only Jerusalem, the city of God, is standing today. Babylon may have gone but its spirit is still with us. However, as we see in the book of Revelation, one day that spirit of pride will be expunged from the earth and the new Jerusalem hold sway.

For reading & meditation – Jeremiah 51:58-64

A strange ending

It was because of the Lord's anger that all this happened to Jerusalem and Judah ...
Jeremiah 52:3

The book of Jeremiah ends in a slightly unexpected way. The story tells how Zedekiah rebelled against the Babylonian oppression, and how Nebuchadnezzar came to put down the rebellion and lay siege to Jerusalem. It ends with the much later release of Jehoiachin who became a recipient of the king's favour. We can be sure that whatever God says will happen. The divine Word has always been fulfilled, is always fulfilled and will always be fulfilled. Nations come and nations go but God's Word endures forever. Hold firmly to it!

For reading & meditation – Jeremiah 52:1-34

Average or excellent?

Some faced jeers and flogging, while still others were chained and put in prison.
Hebrews 11:36

When life seems humdrum, routine and unexciting we must remind ourselves that nothing is more important than doing the work of God. We can opt for the average or we can pursue excellence. Excellence does not always mean the exciting or the adventurous. It means doing God's work faithfully, industriously, and without cutting corners. Has God spoken into your life and given you clear direction concerning the path he wants you to go? Then go for it – and never give up. Doing the work of God faithfully is the excellence he looks for.

For reading & meditation – Hebrews 11:32-40

AUGUST 31

SEPTEMBER

No substitutes

Dear children, keep yourselves from idols.
1 John 5:21

Anything that becomes a centre of interest – greater than the interest we have in God – is an idol. You don't need to reject God openly to be an idolater; you become one simply when you put something or someone other than God at the centre and thus marginalise him. If he is not at the centre then he no longer controls one's life; he just faintly influences it. Idols do more than retard our spiritual maturity; they destroy it. Mark this and mark it well: there can be no ongoing spiritual growth in the life in which idols are present.

For reading & meditation – 1 John 5:1-21

"What a face!"

The Son is ... the exact representation of his being ...
Hebrews 1:3

Jesus is like God in every way – in character, in power and in life. "The Son is ... the exact representation of his being." Jesus does come between us and God, however not as an idol but as a Mediator. He can act as Mediator because he is God. An idol cannot mediate; it can only misrepresent. Behind all idolatry is the desire for God to be visible and understandable. Jesus resolves this issue by fulfilling the longing which gives rise to idolatry but in a way that no idol could ever do. Jesus gives God a face and that face is turned towards us – always.

For reading & meditation – Hebrews 1:1-14

When God is ousted

And he died for all, that those who live should no longer live for themselves ...
2 Corinthians 5:15

God never designed us to be ego-centred; he designed us to be God-centred. This does not mean that he wants us to have a weak ego; rather that our lives should revolve around him instead of around our own selves. When the freshness of God's presence is no longer in the soul (and nothing could be sadder than that) then the result is that we deprave ourselves by carving an idol. And that idol is usually just ourselves. When we lose God we make ourselves God. There can be no greater idolatry than that.

For reading & meditation – 2 Corinthians 5:11-21

The self – writ large

Whoever finds his life will lose it, and whoever loses his life for my sake will find it.
Matthew 10:39

Putting self in the centre rather than God works to our disadvantage because it plays havoc with the self on which we are centring. Every self-centred person is an unhappy and unfulfilled person. When we focus on ourselves then we will go to pieces for life was not designed to work that way. What happens is this: people centre on themselves and seek to have their way and then find they don't like the way they have. They run against this fundamental law: only as we lose ourselves do we find ourselves.

For reading & meditation – Matthew 10:32-42

The steps down

"Leave her alone," Jesus replied. "It was intended that she should save this perfume for ... my burial."
John 12:7

The most powerful example of one whose selfcentredness broke the very self it was attempting to build up is Judas Iscariot. Judas looked for a way to betray Christ (Matt. 26:16). Sin entices with false promises of happiness. The money that seemed to matter so much was flung down and Judas went off and hanged himself. The self that was so demanding and was more interested in getting than giving became impossible to live with. So he hanged the self that at first he tried to save.

For reading & meditation – John 12:1-11

Unable to say "I'm sorry"

Honour one another above yourselves.
Romans 12:10

The self-centred, when frustrated, turn towards themselves in self-pity. They feel that life is hard on them, and in order to deal with the pain of that they use the analgesic of self-pity. They tend to blame everything on other people or things – never themselves. God is powerless to help those who will not yield to him. He will not bludgeon his way into any life – he is too much of a gentleman for that. But given our consent and co-operation then there is nothing he cannot do.

For reading & meditation – Romans 12:1-21

Getting to the root

... you do not have in mind the things of God, but the things of men.
Matthew 16:23

Spiritual maturity has been described as "the process by which we are changed from an unnatural coil around the wrong centre to a natural coil around God as the centre". "Why do we lie? We think it will be of advantage to the self. Why do we become jealous? Because the self is thwarted. Why do we become angry? Because the self is crossed." Counsellors should never forget this when trying to help people. There is no point in dealing with individual sins unless one gets to the root. And the root is very often the unsurrendered self.

For reading & meditation – Matthew 16:21-28

Securing serenity

Though the Lord is on high, he looks upon the lowly, but the proud he knows from afar.
Psalm 138:6

If we centre ourselves on ourselves we won't like ourselves. Destruction and misery are not simply the result of the way of the unrighteous but inherently *in* their ways. The penalty for an unsurrendered self is a self you have to surrender to. If instead of God you choose yourself then you have to live with a self that is shot through with unrighteousness. When you become dependent on God then you become independent of yourself. An unsurrendered self lacks serenity and is alone. Nothing backs you except yourself.

For reading & meditation – Psalm 138:1-8

No half-measures

... every city or household divided against itself will not stand.
Matthew 12:25

The right way to deal with the self is to dedicate it – dedicate it to God in an act of repentance and self-surrender; repentance because you have held on to a self that was designed to work in harmony with God and surrender because that fulfils the eternal law that you must lose yourself in order to find yourself. Until the idol of the self is dethroned we will continue to be immature personalities. So take that inmost idol and smash it once and for all by a deliberate act of self-surrender. Let there be no half-measures. A half-given self is a wholly divided self.

For reading & meditation – Matthew 12:22-37

"Idols" let us down

You shall have no other gods before me.
Exodus 20:3

We are to love people, to be kind to them, but we are not to let them take the place of God in our lives. An idol, we must remember, is something relative that becomes absolute. Once people become absolutes and we look to them rather than to God we start to live dangerously. Many, for example, put their faith in a preacher and look to him more than they look to God. If he stays steady on his pedestal then all is well – everything goes smoothly. He wobbles, or worse, if he falls, then their faith is smashed to pieces.

For reading & meditation – Exodus 20:1-21

The great dilemma

... love your neighbour as yourself.
Matthew 19:19

Although we must not put individuals in the place of God, nevertheless people are important to us. Though we are not to put people in the place of God we are not to live independently of each other. We are to be interdependent. We are social beings and cannot live a full life unless we form relationships. But there is the difficulty: we must relate to others, give to them and in some sense depend on them. However, if we depend on them too much we become stunted.

For reading & meditation – Matthew 19:16-22

Don't be a people-pleaser

There is no fear in love. But perfect love drives out fear ...
1 John 4:18

Many are controlled by the herd instinct to such a degree that they will never go against it – even in the interests of truth and righteousness. They are people-pleasers. We will be loyal to society as long as society is loyal to God, but when the herd goes against what is right and true then we will break with it. As long as our highest loyalty is to God then it is possible to love the herd without being overdependent on it. The herd no longer takes God's place. Jesus' life vividly illustrates this.

For reading & meditation – 1 John 4:7-21

Beware of contagion

And he promised her with an oath, "Whatever you ask I will give you, up to half my kingdom."
Mark 6:23

When we start to accept the standards of the herd then before long our Christian standards become tainted and stained. The religious leaders of Jesus' day could have been the agents of God's new order but they were more concerned about what others thought. Of them it was said: "Everything they do is done for men to see" (Matt. 23:5). They were looking around, not up; angling for the attention of men they missed the signs of the coming kingdom.

For reading & meditation – Mark 6:14-29

"Everybody does it"

May the God who gives endurance and encouragement give you a spirit of unity among yourselves ...
Romans 15:5

When we become truly dependent on God we will not cease to be dependent on others, but we will not be overdependent on them either. If you enter society only for the purpose of getting you will get little. But if you enter in order to contribute then you will get much – as a by-product. You will lose yourself and you will find yourself again. You will grow with the growth of society. Even if others do not respond to your efforts or appreciate your contribution you will be the better for having given. In either case you win.

For reading & meditation – Romans 15:1-13

Lean lightly on things

Let us fix our eyes on Jesus, the author and perfecter of our faith ...
Hebrews 12:2

Enjoy the group but don't become over-dependent on it. Watch that it doesn't become an idol, for you will find that it has feet of clay. Every group is made up of imperfect people – yourself included. Remember if you elevate either a person or a group to the level where they command the adulation due to God alone then you are going to be bitterly disappointed when they let you down. Be willing to be vulnerable but never forget that God and God alone is the One who never disappoints.

For reading & meditation – Hebrews 12:1-13

The purest love

Love the Lord your God with all your heart and with all your soul ...
Mark 12:30

Insecure people – those who do not have a close and dependent relationship with God – are the most vulnerable. In a dependent relationship both people are looking to a person to meet their deepest needs rather than to the Lord Jesus Christ. Thus the other person takes the place of Jesus and becomes an idol. Some Christians take the text "God is love" and turn it around to mean "Love is God." The idol of "another" has gathered everything to itself. The consequence of this is that both are immature persons. Loved ones can be idols that push out God.

For reading & meditation – Mark 12:28-34

Watch out!

Watch out! Be on your guard against all kinds of greed ...
Luke 12:15

There is a terrible attachment in the normal human heart to "things". In one sense it is understandable; we live in a material world where we depend on material things and it would be foolish to say we can ignore them. Our interest in worldly goods can quickly elbow out concern about spiritual issues, and if this becomes the case we will find ourselves growing grasping, greedy and covetous. One of the saddest states that a follower of Christ can fall into is allowing things to master his or her life.

For reading & meditation – Luke 12:13-21

"I am richer than you"

Do not store up for yourselves treasures on earth ...
But store up ... treasures in heaven ...
Matthew 6:19-20

Material things are regarded as the greatest source of happiness in life only by those who do not have them. Things are incapable of meeting the deepest hunger of the heart. Our standards of value today are frankly materialistic. "They must be," people retort, "it is a material world." *Only* a material world? *Pre-eminently* a material world? Communism and capitalism say by implication: "Things are all that matter." God says: "Things are your servants, use them."

For reading & meditation – Matthew 6:19-34

The great danger

What good is it for a man to gain the whole world, yet forfeit his soul?
Mark 8:36

Our Lord knew a minimum of material things was necessary without which life would be difficult, if not impossible. No one can accuse the Saviour of ignoring people's needs. He fed the hungry, had a special concern for the poor and encouraged generosity among those to whom he preached. When things become the chief purpose of living, when possessions are seen as life's greatest good, when men and woman work in order to get rather than give, then all of live is in danger – the integrity of the human soul, the well-being of the community, the soundness of all human life.

For reading & meditation – Mark 8:31-38

SEPTEMBER 19

The final test

They are worthless, the objects of mockery; when their judgment comes, they will perish.
Jeremiah 10:15

An idol such as wealth can give the appearance of security but all it does is "break down when the test arrives". The inability of things to satisfy the human soul has been demonstrated in every age yet people are still caught by the lure of acquisition. Material things often bring cares, griefs and deep unease. We must face the fact that the final "test" of life is death. How does the idol of wealth – of *things* – stand up to the test which death brings? It breaks down. You can't take things with you. The idol of wealth is concerned with this life only. Thus it breaks down at the final test.

For reading & meditation – Jeremiah 10:11-25

A safe journey

... that we might ... ask (God) for a safe journey for us and our children, with all our possessions.
Ezra 8:21

At first sight it seems as if Ezra's prayer asking God for a safe journey for the people and their possessions is a self-centred one. But not so. The main purpose of the prayer was that they might return to Jerusalem and rebuild the Temple. The matter of a safe journey for them and their possessions was incidental. Their real concern was the glory of God. It is pointless to ask for protection for your possessions if God's glory is not the ultimate goal.

For reading & meditation – Ezra 8:15-36

At his disposal

... whether ... the world or life or death or the present or the future – all are yours, and you are of Christ, and Christ is of God.
1 Corinthians 3:22-23

Whether or not we acknowledge it we do not actually own our possessions; we are only in possession of our possessions for a brief period. Scripture tells me that everything belongs to Christ and because I belong to him everything he has belongs to me. If in reality we do not own our possessions then we must have the sense to say to God: "I am not the owner; I am the ower. Teach me how to work out that relationship for your honour and glory." Since we belong to God all we have belongs to God. It must therefore be at his disposal.

For reading & meditation – 1 Corinthians 3:1-23

"Unpurchasable men"

... get rid of all moral filth and the evil that is so prevalent, and humbly accept the word planted in you ...
James 1:21

Society will quickly fall apart unless it has a nucleus of men and women of integrity – men and women whom *nothing* can buy. Materialism has the sinister tendency to barter for the soul and filch integrity, to corrupt a person's desires and cause rot to a whole community. Our Lord made this a constant emphasis in his ministry. He warned the men and women of his day by parable and by precept of the awful consequences of making an idol out of things. He himself lived, in comparative poverty in order to illustrate that fullness of life was possible with a minimum of this world's goods.

For reading & meditation – James 1:19-27

Virtues that vitiate

And whatever you do ... do it all in the name of the Lord Jesus ...
Colossians 3:17

We now consider another idol that can easily take the place of God in our lives – *virtues*. To some it may sound strange that our virtues can vitiate our spirituality, yet it happens when we put a quality of which we are proud in place of God. The good then pushes out the best. Be sure of this: the Almighty is ever pressing to gain possession of the inmost shrine of our being and he will not permit any intruder to occupy the centre, not even a virtue. The thought that we can be in bondage to a virtue may be hard to grasp, but we can.

For reading & meditation – Colossians 3:1-17

Proud of our humility?

Who is wise and understanding ...? Let him show it by ... deeds done in the humility that comes from wisdom.
James 3:13

It is possible to develop a virtue and then rest on that virtue instead of resting on God. The virtue therefore becomes an idol – a substitute for God. "The more you grow spiritually the more pride becomes a danger." How true. Pride is a parasite that has weakened many a person's character and turned a virtue into a vice. Let us be careful that we do not fall into the trap of putting more confidence in our virtues than we do in God. True humility is largely something of which we are unconscious – a by-product of dwelling close to God. If we are conscious of it we probably do not possess it.

For reading & meditation – James 3:1-18

Punctuality and pride

Do not worship any other god, for the Lord whose name is Jealous, is a jealous God.
Exodus 34:14

Punctuality has been defined as "having respect for other people's time." Those who are always late for appointments and are not careful with time create great difficulties for other people. They show by their actions their true feelings concerning others. Some psychologists maintain that the dynamic behind being constantly late is unconscious anger. The anger (so they say) is being let out gently in ways that are not too anti-social. Well, be that as it may, punctuality too can have within it the parasite of pride.

For reading & meditation – Exodus 34:1-14

The thirst for praise

Be careful not to do your "acts of righteousness" before men, to be seen by them.
Matthew 6:1

It is perilously possible that our virtues become a "god" for us – a "god" from which we seek to gain affirmation instead of drawing on the one true God. It's pleasant to be affirmed and it's encouraging when the good things we do are acknowledged, but it is so easy for our service for God to be spoiled by our thirst for personal praise. When our longing to be praised is greater than our desire to serve God whether or not that service is recognised then we are dangerously close to making it a "god".

For reading & meditation – Matthew 6:1-4

Dutifulness

*But his delight is in the law of the Lord,
and on his law he meditates day and night.*
Psalm 1:2

There are people who are virtuous out of a sense of duty; because it's right. The root problem in the human heart is *misplaced dependency*. A fine Christian had an exceptionally keen sense of duty and one day the suggestion was put to him that he might be governed more by a sense of duty than dependence on God. To his credit he saw it at once. He prayed: " I don't want to be held together by duty; I want to be held together by you." He continued to be a dutiful person but his dutifulness came from his God-dependence rather than self-dependence.

For reading & meditation – Psalm 1:1-6

Something missing!

Trust in the Lord with all your heart and lean not on your own understanding ...
Proverbs 3:5

Discipline is definitely needed in our lives if we are to be good disciples of the Master. Very often "free grace" has been preached in such a way that character has been weakened. Paul warns against this in these words: "You, my brothers, were called to be free. But do not use your freedom to indulge the sinful nature ..." (Gal. 5:13). Here liberty had become licence. Discipline was needed. Nothing must take the place of God, not even a virtue. *Dependency* plus discipline makes dependable disciples.

For reading & meditation – Proverbs 3:1-12

Indulgent praying

And when you pray, do not be like the hypocrites ...
Matthew 6:5

Could anything be more morally excellent than prayerfulness? But even prayer can become an idol if we depend on our praying ability rather than on God. "Sometimes you leave other people not wanting to follow you in prayer because they may not have such skill with words as you do. Is there a "god" in this for you?" If prayerfulness is one of your Christian qualities and you are one of God's intercessors then rejoice in it and be glad. But don't depend on your prowess in prayer. Depend only on God.

For reading & meditation – Matthew 6:5-15

OCTOBER

Self-atonement

... we also rejoice in God through our Lord Jesus Christ, through whom we have now received reconciliation.
Romans 5:11

Many involve themselves in an act of penance in order to clear the guilt that has arisen in their soul over some spiritual violation; they depend on the act of penance rather than on Christ's atoning sufferings on Calvary and thus substitute their own atonement for his. This tendency to make amends for one's wrongdoings must be watched most carefully for many Christians fall into the trap of believing that they can atone for sin by an act of penance. "Our very penance needs to be repented of." It does if it depends more on self than the Saviour.

For reading & meditation – Romans 5:1-11

An escape from guilt

When I kept silent, my bones wasted away through my groaning all day long.
Psalm 32:3

Counsellors have often commented on the interesting fact that when a man or woman falls into sin and a sense of guilt begins to spread through the personality some inner mechanism goes to work to help them escape it or dissolve it. Some (albeit unconsciously) try to escape from guilt by developing an illness. "If you won't deal with the discomfort in your soul then deal with it in your body." Psalm 32:1-11 was written by David before he confessed his adultery with Bathsheba. Clearly he speaks of the physical effects of his unconfessed sin.

For reading & meditation – Psalm 32:1-11

Other forms of retreat

... the younger son ... set off for a distant country and there squandered his wealth in wild living.
Luke 15:13

The soul is adept at helping us escape from the feelings that arise whenever a moral principle has been violated. Some try to escape in more overt ways, for instance by drinking alcohol to dull the conscience. But over every escape route is a sign that reads: "No way through." Guilt can be assuaged but it can never be properly removed through self-pity, illness or any other form of escapism. You can't make a halfway house a home.

For reading & meditation – Luke 15:15-32

The circle of offence

Therefore, if you ... remember that your brother has something against you ... go and be reconciled to your brother ...
Matthew 5:23-24

Carl Jung, the psychologist said: "As soon as man was capable of conceiving the idea of sin, repressions arose." He added: "We conceal it even from ourselves." If someone has committed an offence against God and another person then both God and the other person must be approached. If the violation is against God and God alone then seek his forgiveness only. If it is against God and someone else then seek the forgiveness of God and the individual. Limit the confession to the circle of offence.

For reading & meditation – Matthew 5:21-26

Jonah – the impenitent

Pick me up and throw me into the sea ... and it will become calm.
Jonah 1:12

Probably one of the clearest illustrations of someone resorting to penance, as opposed to repentance, is Jonah. Penance is an attempt to make atonement for sin by an act which often causes suffering. Repentance is sorrow for sin leading to a turning away from it and the discovery of release in Christ. There is a genuine place for penance in the Christian life – the story of Zaccheus shows this. But far too often penance is a substitute for repentance. This is how it was with Jonah. He mistook remorse for repentance – a mistake made by millions.

For reading & meditation – Jonah 1:1-17

Did Jonah repent?

I said, "I have been banished from your sight; yet I will look again towards your holy temple."
Jonah 2:4

There is something about human nature that makes us want to do something to remedy our spiritual deficiencies rather than trust in the grace and power of God. We have to recognise that in ourselves we are powerless to atone. Though we must do what we can to right wrongs, the action of putting things right must not be seen as atonement. God has provided atonement for us through Christ's redeeming sacrifice on the cross and we must be careful that we do nothing to by pass that, either in thought or in deed. An act of penance may be needed in addition to repentance but must never replace it.

For reading & meditation – Jonah 2:1-10

"Look what you made me do!"

Jonah ... waited to see what would happen to the city.
Jonah 3:5

The unrepentant always blame other. Jonah blamed God. And watch how he continued to punish himself. He wanted God to take away his life. This put him in control. He was the one giving the orders. When there is insincere repentance then the tendency is to rely on substitutes, to hop from one subterfuge to another. Jonah wanted to die because he had never died to Jonah. He had never truly repented. When the curtain falls, Jonah is still running. Be careful that when the curtain falls on your life your situation is not like that of Jonah.

For reading & meditation – Jonah 3:1-4:11

OCTOBER 7

"A celestial Santa Claus"

... anyone who comes to him must believe that he exists ...
Hebrews 11:6

We can oust the true God from the centre of our lives and adopt a different type of idol: *by clinging to a wrong concept of him*. "... anyone who comes to him must believe that he exists" ... means more than that we must reject atheism. It means we must accept God as he is, not as we would like him to be. God made us in his image and we have returned the compliment by making him in ours. Many Christians do just this. Unable to accept God as he is, they form a concept of him that is more acceptable to them, little realising that by doing so they are actually substituting imagination for revelation, and that is idolatry.

For reading & meditation – Hebrews 11:1-10

Metal and mental images

... they cut a tree out of the forest,
and a craftsman shapes it with his chisel!
Jeremiah 10:3

"Metal images are the consequence of mental images." In his denunciation of idolatry, whether the image being venerated is a metal or a mental one, God declares: "Don't miscalculate my reaction. I, the Lord your God, am a jealous God." With all the intensity and integrity of his being he insists on his rightful place at the centre of the universe and on the throne of his people's hearts. He will resist with omnipotent power anything that seeks to prevent him occupying that central position.

For reading & meditation – Jeremiah 10:1-16

OCTOBER 9

In spirit and in truth

God is spirit, and his worshippers
must worship in spirit and in truth.
John 4:24

Once we try to remake God in our own image, once we attempt to change our concept of him from who he really is to how we want him to be, we find ourselves estranged from the real world and divorced from truth. We are in denial. We are living with an illusion. Hence when we try to worship God we are not worshipping the real God but a caricature of him. We are Christian idolaters. Accepting God as he is means facing up to the fact that some things he does are beyond explanation and are a complete and utter mystery. But we decide to trust him nevertheless.

For reading & meditation – John 4:1-24

True worship

For we cannot do anything against the truth, but only for the truth.
2 Corinthians 13:8

"True worship," said C.S. Lewis in *Reflections on the Psalms*, "is inner health made audible." C.S. Lewis also said this about worship: "In the process of worship God communicates his presence to men." God cannot fully come in to us except through worship and we cannot fully communicate with God unless we worship in spirit and in *truth*. No truth – no worship. We remain stunted and immature if we refuse to face reality. Sometimes we might wish God would act differently but we must watch that a wish does not develop into a demand.

For reading & meditation – 2 Corinthians 13:1-14

Fastening onto a fantasy

If we claim to be without sin, we deceive ourselves and the truth is not in us.
1 John 1:8

"If we refuse to admit that we are sinners, then we live in a world of illusion and truth becomes a stranger to us. But if we freely admit that we have sinned, we find God utterly reliable and straightforward" (vv. 8-9). In order to live effectively in this world we must admit that whatever is, is. The avoidance of reality brings about a diminution of our personalities and moves us into a world of illusion. A serious thing takes place when we do not accept God as he is but seek to change him into someone with whom we can live more comfortably: we put in God's place an image we have manufactured ourselves.

For reading & meditation – 1 John 1:1-10

Three ways to "see" God

No-one has ever seen God, but God the One and Only, who is at the Father's side, has made him known.
John 1:18

We cannot worship God properly unless we accept him as he is. True worship, according to C.S. Lewis implies a two-way process: "In the process of worship God communicates himself to men." We will not be able to work or witness for God either unless we accept him as he is. Inevitably the way we see God will govern the way we will talk about him. Our perceptions determine our communications. There are only three ways we can see him. One, as he is. Two, as we imagine him to be. Three, as we would like him to be.

For reading & meditation – John 1:1-18

Jesus' other Name

I am the way and the truth and the life. No-one comes to the Father except through me.
John 14:6

Often people worship an idol because they want something that is get-at-able, tangible, approachable. Jesus is all these – and how! He is *Immanuel*, God with us. God did not give us a proposition in order to explain reality; he gave us a Person. And what a Person! Jesus is the way that can be trodden. He trod it. Jesus is the truth. His truth rings true everywhere. Jesus is the life that can be lived. He lived it. When reality renders its verdict it points to Jesus. Nothing can be truer than this final quote from E. Stanley Jones: "Reality – whose other name is Jesus."

For reading & meditation – John 14:1-14

God at our level

O Lord, God of Israel, there is no God like you in heaven above or on earth below ...
1 Kings 8:23

R*eductionism* imposes limits on divine transcendence and contributes to the shrinking of God in our minds. There are some Christians who like to think of their church building as the place where God is confined because they can then keep him in there, visit him once a week like a sick relative, and run their lives the way *they* want to. This destroys reverence by making God less than he is. It is true that he came down to our level in the incarnation, but immanence was not achieved at the cost of transcendence.

For reading & meditation – 1 Kings 8:22-30

A great mystery

He who descended is the very one who ascended higher than all the heavens, in order to fill the whole universe.
Ephesians 4:10

God's coming to this earth in the form of a man is the event that marks Christianity as being distinct from every other faith. He came to set the gospel over against human need whether that need be in followers of this religion or that religion or of no religion. The Son of God became the Son of Man in order that the sons of men might become the sons of God. Our Lord who became man ascended to the Father and now as a *man* he fills the whole universe. Because of the incarnation his immanence is incontrovertible. And so also is his transcendence.

For reading & meditation – Ephesians 4:1-16

OCTOBER 16

The fine line

... you ought to say, "If it is the Lord's will, we will live and do this or that.
James 4:15

It would appear that each culture and generation makes its own attempt to reduce God to a size where he can be manipulated. God does indeed concern himself with his people and is interested in blessing them, sometimes in material ways. Prayer says: "Lord, this is what I would like to happen, but I understand you see things from a different perspective so I submit everything to your judgement." Demandingness says: "Lord, this is what I want to happen and so let it be according to the word of faith that is now on my lips." There is a fine line between faith and demandingness and many Christians are not able to recognise it.

For reading & meditation – James 4:1-17

OCTOBER 17

God in a box

... Uzzah reached out and took hold of the ark of God ... The Lord's anger burned against Uzzah ...
2 Samuel 6:5-6

Why should God's anger have burned towards Uzzah? Uzzah was guilty of having a limited view of God's transcendence. If we could have looked into his heart I think we might have found that his understanding of God was of a being confined to a box. Such a view of God produces a slow spiritual death. In Uzzah's case it also produced physical death when in raising his hand he really tipped his hand. Nothing insults God more than when we assume that we can carry him rather than accepting that he carries us.

For reading & meditation – 2 Samuel 6:1-11

Who carries who?

... I am God, and there is no other;
I am God and there is none like me.
Isaiah 46:9

When we think we are in control of God then we are nothing more than idolaters. We are attempting to manage the unmanageable, to control the uncontrollable. If our understanding of God is that we can carry him then we are attempting to be in control. Perhaps I want to make God manageable so that I can put him where I want him and where he won't intrude too much on my life. If I am seeking to control God then I am trying to make myself God. Think about that, and drop the attempt as quickly as possible.

For reading & meditation – Isaiah 46:1-13

OCTOBER 19

Subtle self-deification

Do you not know? Have you not heard?
The Lord is the everlasting God ...
Isaiah 40:28

"If I am seeking to control God then I am trying to make myself God." Let's think for a moment about the repercussions of that in our lives. If I am attempting to make myself God I will then worship my creator – myself. Like the self-made man I will get terribly upset if things do not go the way I think they should go. We are not God. If we think we are then God help us.

For reading & meditation – Isaiah 40:18-31

"Beware of God"

... for our "God is a consuming fire."
Hebrews 12:29

We Christians live in an atmosphere where God has been brought too near. We are so taken up with his immanence – his nearness and availability – that we tend to ignore the fact of his transcendence. God is not someone to be managed but someone who is high and lifted up and who deserves to be worshipped. We need to be delivered from the idolatry of trying to manage him and instead let him manage us. "Without real transcendence, there is no weighty God to fall before, only a co-operative God to celebrate."

For reading & meditation – Hebrews 12:14-29

A substitute love

He answered: "Love the Lord your God ..." and , "Love your neighbour ..."
Luke 10:27

When an expert in the law stood up and asked Jesus what he had to do to inherit eternal life, Jesus did not say "You must be just" or "You must be kind." Suppose he had singled out a good quality instead of the highest. Had he done so the history of humanity from that moment on would have been different. He sounded a clarion note: "You shall *love*." The ages were thirsting for that word for from the beginning that is what we were made to do – to love. The first obligation God lays on every one of us is to love. And not simply to love in the way we understand love but as God loves.

For reading & meditation – Luke 10:25-37

An ethical revolution

Love does not delight in evil
but rejoices with the truth.
1 Corinthians 13:6

Christians adopted the Greek word *agape* and gave it a distinctively Christian sense. That word, when filled with Christian meaning, introduces the most revolutionary idea ever presented to the mind of man. Anders Nygren, a devout Christian says: "The Christian idea of love ... involves a revolution in ethical outlook without parallel in the history of ethics." As Christians we simply must understand this revolution arising from the Christian takeover of the word *agape* so that it grips and controls us as it did the Early Church.

For reading & meditation – 1 Corinthians 13:1-13

Eros and agape

... make my joy complete by being likeminded, having the same love, being one in spirit and purpose.
Philippians 2:2

The New Testament writers never once used the word *eros*, and apart from a few occasions when they spoke of *philia* (affection, fondness) they consistently used the word *agape*. *Eros*, generally speaking, is the love that loves for what it can gain from that love. It turns everything – even God – into a means to an end. *Eros* loves because it sees in its object of love something that can bring satisfaction in return. Here the issues are drawn. As Christians we must decide on which side we will line up for we have to be on one side or the other.

For reading & meditation – Philippians 2:1-18

Three views of the soul

All have turned away, they have together become worthless ...
Romans 3:12

The soul is naturally Christian. It is made for God and functions effectively only when he is in it. If the soul were naturally pagan it would be uncomfortable and ill at ease when indwelt by Christ. If the soul were naturally pagan why should it be punished for its pagan ways? It would be unjust to punish it for living according to its nature. There is something in us all that feels evil is evil; we witness to it as being unnatural. The love that God put into us at the beginning has been twisted by sin. We can still love but not in the way God loves. Our love needs a homecoming. It needs to be converted.

For reading & meditation – Romans 3:1-20

"Conversion of our loves"

Again Jesus said, "Simon son of John, do you truly love me?"
John 21:16

Can *eros* be changed into *agape*? Self-surrender involves surrendering love of the self, and when self-surrender takes place then the love which is inherently in the self is untangled from the self and fastened onto God who is *Agape*. If evil is perversion of the good then conversion is conversion from perversion. Those who are converted, truly converted, begin to love the right things for the right reasons and for the right ends. Loving with the right kind of love is *agape*. It is what we were made for. Nothing more, nothing less.

For reading & meditation – John 21:15-25

Put out your candles

We love because he first loved us.
1 John 4:19

Isn't *agape* too high for us to attain? How can we love as God loves? Isn't that just for saints and exceptional people? "We love because he first loved us." Note the word *because*. To have God's love in us requires not striving but receiving. When we focus on the fact that we are loved by the world's greatest Lover and open ourselves to that love it flows like Niagara's waters into our souls. You don't need to strive; you simply have to let it come in. Open your eyes and the light comes in. Open your heart and love comes in.

For reading & meditation – 1 John 4:7-21

Loving God for "me"

For Christ's love compels us, because we are convinced that one died for all ...
2 Corinthians 5:14

Human love (largely) loves for what it can gain. It loves people for what they can give in return. God too can be loved for what he gives rather than for who he is. We make him a means to our end. He saves us from trouble, heals us of our sicknesses, gives us success in life, blesses our business, and provides us with a heaven hereafter. When we approach God like this and function in our daily lives from this perspective we are substituting for *agape* love our own self-centred love, and this substitution is one of the greatest idolatries of all.

For reading & meditation – 2 Corinthians 5:11-21

Nothing higher

My command is this: Love each other as I have loved you.
John 15:12

Two thousand years ago, however, God sent his Son into our world, the Son who is "the exact representation of his being" (Heb. 1:3), and demonstrated for us what *agape* is really like. "Love each other as I have loved you." This raised the commandment from the Old Testament to the New, from law to grace. He loved individuals not as they loved each other but with a different type and quality of love – a love that required a different word to express it: *agape*. But that word would have been fairly devoid of meaning had not Jesus filled it with the purest and deepest love this planet has ever seen.

For reading & meditation – John 15:1-17

Misrepresenting God

By this all men will know that you are my disciples, if you love one another.
John 13:35

If we say we love but all the world sees is a love that is self-centred, egocentric and is out for what it can get then in effect we are conveying that God has that attitude – that he loves for what he can gain. God is then misrepresented by our representation. Instead the world should see us exhibiting a love that says: "I don't want to get, I want to give." Anything less than *agape* or anything other than *agape* is a substitution. Let us have done with the idolatry of a substitute love and allow God's *agape* to penetrate our souls until we too are filled with all the fullness of God.

For reading & meditation – John 13:18-38

"Him only"

Then the devil left him, and
angels came and attended him.
Matthew 4:11

The list of things to which we can become devoted to the exclusion of God himself is endless; consider also, for example, greed, covetousness, nationalism and race, religious ceremonies, and so on. When Jesus said to the devil following the third temptation "Serve him only" the devil, we are told, left him. The devil could not stand the "him only" attitude and decision. So from now on let there be no trucking with idols, no substitutes, no lesser gods, no god-shelf on which Jesus stands as one among many other gods. Sweep every idol from your life. There must be no substitute for him. Let your resolve be "him only".

For reading & meditation – Matthew 4:1-11

NOVEMBER

David – the giant-killer

The Lord ... will deliver me
from the hand of this Philistine.
1 Samuel 17:37

Day after day Goliath paraded along the slopes of the Valley of Elah, bellowing out challenges to the Israelites. On to the scene came a young shepherd boy by the name of David. He could not believe the way his fellow Israelites – God's chosen people – allowed themselves to be intimidated by Goliath. With a sling, a small stone and a mighty confidence in God the young shepherd boy ended the giant's reign of terror once and for all. Are there any "giants" looming large on the horizon right now? The chances are some are threatening your life at this very moment.

For reading & meditation – 1 Samuel 17:1-58

The Spirit's expertise

The weapons we fight with are not the weapons of the world.
2 Corinthians 10:4

Don't run away with the idea that because David slew Goliath with just one stone set in a sling, slaying a giant is a simple matter. It requires great skill, great dedication and great discipline. The weapons of our warfare, as Scripture says, may not be carnal, but they are weapons nevertheless and are effective only in the hands of dedicated and disciplined operators. Using the sling of faith and the stone of truth is less cumbersome than wielding a sword, a club or a spear, but it requires just as much expertise. That expertise, however, is born not of the flesh but of the Spirit.

For reading & meditation – 2 Corinthians 10:1-18

"The Spectre on the Brocken"

"Have faith in God," Jesus answered.
Mark 11:22

Some fears are as unsubstantial as the "The Spectre on the Brocken". For centuries it was rumoured by people who lived in the Harz mountains that a giant lived on the summit. Before long they realised what was happening. The ghostly and terrifying spectre which people saw on the peak was nothing but a distorted image of themselves. Some of our terrors are like that. They are the result of a diseased imagination. So look over your fears and separate the real from the imaginary. You will find that most fears exist only in the imagination.

For reading & meditation – Mark 11:20-33

No false remedies

Woe to those who go down to Egypt for help ... but do not look to the Holy One of Israel ...
Isaiah 31:1

Fear, we must understand, is quite different from anxiety. Anxiety is a vague and unspecified apprehension; fear always has a specific object. Every diversion, whether it is drink, overeating, illicit sex, gambling or entertainment, are cul-de-sacs – dead ends. They lead only to deeper difficulty. So make up your mind not to take any false routes to escape fear. No subterfuge can ever be a refuge. We need to close all wrong doors so that the right one is more obvious. When we see the right door – Jesus – we can then walk boldly through it into release.

For reading & meditation – Isaiah 31:1-9

Open-eyed honesty

... be clear minded and self-controlled
so that you can pray.
1 Peter 4:7

The verse that most clearly expresses the need to face things rather than evade them is Matthew 24:6: "You will hear of wars ... but see to it that you are not alarmed." In other words, confront fears and don't be scared. Our Lord is the One who is speaking here. His way is the way of open-eyed honesty. Learn the art of prayer, for fears dissolve in its powerful atmosphere. One of the greatest fears that prayer destroys is the fear of the future. And it destroys it by assuring us that though we do not know what the future holds, we are held by the One who knows the future.

For reading & meditation – 1 Peter 4:1-11

"The three omni's"

I will say of the Lord, "He is my refuge and my fortress, my God, in whom I trust."
Psalm 91:2

We are always in God's presence, we are all attached to a God who is omnipotent, omniscient and omnipresent. *Omnipotence* means God is all-powerful. And he makes his strength available for our needs. Take next his *omniscience*. This means that he is all-knowing. As we gain strength to face our fears by leaning on the all-powerful God so we also gain strength from his wisdom. Then third, *omnipresence*. This means God is present everywhere. I cannot go where he is not. When we see God as he is and our attachment to him deepens then fears are reduced to their proper size.

For reading & meditation – Psalm 91:1-16

Fear – not from God

For God did not give us a spirit of timidity, but a spirit of power, of love and of selfdiscipline.
2 Timothy 1:7

Without going overboard on this matter of rebuking the devil (as some Christians appear to do), be aware that the Holy Spirit indwells you and his strong voice will overcome your weakness and defeat Satan's work in your life. Calmly and confidently stand up to that devilish fear in the authority which is yours in Christ. It wasn't just the sling and the stone that caused Goliath to fall. It was the sling, the stone and the mighty Name of Jehovah. Take your stand now against every crippling fear in your life and resist the work of Satan in Christ's mighty and powerful Name.

For reading & meditation – 2 Timothy 1:1-12

"Fear not!"

There is no fear in love. But perfect love drives out fear ...
1 John 4:18

Our Lord taught his disciples that fear (properly understood) has only one object – God. "I will show you whom you should fear," he said to his disciples on one occasion. "Fear him who ... has power to throw you into hell" (Luke 12:5). One of our Lord's favourite phrases was "Fear not." Again and again it rang out: "Fear not." How was it that Christ was so free of fear? Because of his complete confidence in his Father who was on the throne, and knowledge that all his purposes were wise and good. Assured of this his mind had no crevices in which fear could hide.

For reading & meditation – 1 John 4:7-21

"It is good for me!"

My soul is overwhelmed with sorrow to the point of death.
Matthew 26:38

In the face of the most awful thing that could befall him Jesus probably told himself something like this: "If my Father allows this then it is good for me!" We see that most clearly in Gethsemane. "Shall I not drink the cup the Father has given me?" Jesus asked (John 18:11). Men were about to lift him up on a cross but he saw that his Father had a purpose even in that. Jesus knew that his Father who was great in creation was mighty in transformation also. These two facts alone were enough to keep Jesus free from fear. They are enough for us too.

For reading & meditation – Matthew 26:36-46

Two kinds of jealousy

Anger is cruel and fury overwhelming,
but who can stand before jealousy?
Proverbs 27:4

An instance of good jealousy is found in the words: "I, the Lord your God, am a jealous God" (Ex. 20:5). Because God loved his people with an abounding and pure love he was jealous for them. He was not jealous for himself but jealous for them – for their highest good. The more common form of jealousy is as hateful as the other is praiseworthy. You love something or someone very much and desire to possess it or them completely. But the thing or person you love slips out of your hands into the possession of another. You then begin to experience the gnawing pangs of jealousy.

For reading & meditation – Proverbs 27:1-11

Jealousy's peculiarity

... for jealousy arouses a husband's fury, and he will show no mercy when he takes revenge.
Proverbs 6:34

Jealousy is the dislike that turns to bitterness when someone attracts more attention than you, or has sipped the waters of success more deeply than you have. Charles Swindoll puts it like this: "Envy begins with empty hands mourning for what it doesn't have. Jealousy begins with full hands but is threatened by the loss. It is the pain of losing what I have to someone else, in spite of all my efforts to keep it." One thing is sure – the giant of jealousy is a killer. You must make up your mind in God's name to kill it. If you don't, it will eventually kill you.

For reading & meditation – Proverbs 6:20-35

"A mental cancer"

... on Cain and his offering he did not look with favour. So Cain was very angry, and his face was downcast.
Genesis 4:5

Jesus told the parable we call "The Prodigal Son." The younger brother squandered the money given to him by his father in riotous living. His sin could be described as a sin of the flesh. The elder brother had a different kind of problem. His sin was jealousy – a sin of the spirit. And when the curtain comes down on that immortal story we see the man who sinned in the flesh being forgiven and inside the father's house, while the man who sinned in the spirit is holding on to his jealousy and remains outside. Jealousy distorts and throws everything out of focus.

For reading & meditation – Genesis 4:1-16

Jealous? Me?

I fear that there may be quarrelling, jealousy, outbursts of anger ...
2 Corinthians 12:20

How can the giant of jealousy be slain? First we have to admit that it exists. Of course it can be humiliating to admit to things in our lives that we wish were not there. And pride can play its part in this too. Pride rebels at the idea that we can be jealous of another person, especially when we perceive them as being unworthy of comparison with ourselves. Jealous? Me? Of her? Of him? So we brush aside the fact that we may be jealous and go on for a few more years denying the deadly thing which is ruining our lives.

For reading & meditation – 2 Corinthians 12:11-21

Organs of one another

Now you are the body of Christ,
and each one of you is a part of it.
1 Corinthians 12:27

Once we have admitted that jealousy is a problem in our lives, what should we then do? Look on jealousy as self-centredness. Jealousy is "envy born of some deep love of self," so you must realise that if you are a jealous person you are a self-centred person. Most of our problems in the Christian life have their roots in an unsurrendered ego. We can be saved but not yet fully surrendered. If jealousy is a problem in your life, repent of holding on to self-centredness for so long, and make a complete surrender to God.

For reading & meditation – 1 Corinthians 12:12-31

Right comparisons

When Peter saw him, he asked,
"Lord, what about him?"
John 21:21

Constantly comparing ourselves with others can do us a great deal of harm spiritually. If we conclude we are better than those with whom we compare ourselves we can be trapped into pride. If we conclude we are inferior to them we can be trapped into envy. To compare ourselves with Jesus is a healthy spiritual discipline, and one that has been practised throughout the centuries by those who have known the Lord intimately. So keep your eyes fixed on Jesus and satisfy this impulse to make comparisons in a way that will yield for your life spiritual gain.

For reading & meditation – John 21:15-25

"Gaze on him alone"

... that man who was with you ... is baptising, and everyone is going to him.
John 3:26

Once we are rightly related to God, and we are caught up in the fact that Infinite Love and Infinite Wisdom are guiding our course, how can we want to change places with others? In his will is our peace. When we have established a right relationship with God (the key to it all) then he takes from us the eagerness for human praise which is the cause of so much jealousy. It is the intense longing for admiration which leads many people into this sin. They want the applause, the flattery – this is how they come to envy the people who get it.

For reading & meditation – John 3:22-36

Run-away desires

For from within ... come evil thoughts ... greed, malice, deceit, lewdness ...
Mark 7:21-22

Another giant that overshadows the life of many a Christian is that of lewd desires. Desire, as such, is one of the God-given forces of the personality. Without it life would be dull and sluggish. But when desire becomes our master rather than our servant then something has to be done about it. Buddha tried to help people overcome desire by cutting the root of desire itself. But you cannot cure the ills of life by eliminating an integral part of life. We can't stop lustful thoughts arising in our minds but with God's help we can stop them residing there.

For reading & meditation – Mark 7:14-23

A judge's downfall

His father and mother replied. "... Must you go to the uncircumcised Philistines to get a wife?"
Judges 14:3

One preacher described Samson as a "he-man with a she-weakness". He became so preoccupied with his lustful desires that the time came when he didn't even know the Lord had departed from him (16:20). The result of Samson's lustful affairs is known to us all. The strong man was taken captive, had his eyes gouged out, his hair shaved and finished up as a grinder in a Philistine prison. His eyes would never wander again. Sin binds, sin blinds, and sin grinds. Lust is a flame no one dare fan. You'll get burned if you do.

For reading & meditation – Judges 14:1-20

"No respecter of persons"

For God did not call us to be impure, but to live a holy life.
1 Thessalonians 4:7

No one is immune from sexual temptation. You are not, and I am not. Lust is no respecter of persons. Its alluring voice can inveigle the most intelligent minds and persuade its victims to believe a lie. The silver-tongued orator of Rome, Mark Anthony was so consumed with lust that his tutor once shouted in disgust: "O Marcus! O colossal child ... able to conquer the world but unable to resist a temptation!" Men and women reading these lines today are in a similar position. Who can save them from this condition? Let them hear the good news – Jesus can.

For reading & meditation – 1 Thessalonians 4:1-12

The law of the sex life

... a man is a slave to whatever has mastered him.
2 Peter 2:19

We can live without sex but we cannot live without food or water. Bring the fact of sex into the open in your thinking and at the same time invite Christ to guide your thoughts on this issue. Settle it once and for all that sex is not your master – Christ is. If you put sex first it will corrupt your whole life. If you put Jesus first he will co-ordinate your whole life. Sex will then be your servant and not your master. The law of the sex life is this: He that saves his sex life – puts it first – shall lose his life. There are no exceptions and no exemptions.

For reading & meditation – 2 Peter 2:4-22

Our reply to lust

... sin shall not be your master, because you are not under law, but under grace.
Romans 6:14

Victory or defeat depends on the skill and speed with which a sensual thought is managed in the mind. If a man or woman turns their thoughts to Christ, thinks about him, talks to him, and makes this a firm routine whenever tempted, it will save their vagrant thoughts from escalating into lust. One writer puts it like this: "When Lust suggests a rendezvous, send Jesus Christ as your representative." Remind yourself of the verse before us today, which tells us that we are united with Christ. You are no longer a slave to a "giant". You have a new Master.

For reading & meditation – Romans 6:1-14

One law for Christians

Love the Lord your God with all your heart and with all your soul and with all your mind ...
Mark 12:30

You can expel one desire only by a higher desire, one passion by a stronger passion. Let the love of Christ, therefore, be the love that consumes all lesser loves. All the prohibitions against the wrong use of sexual desire will not save you unless the love of Christ is at the centre. The Christian has just one law: thou shalt love. And love becomes the fulfilling of the law. God has placed a thirst for himself deep in every heart, and unless that thirst is quenched by him then we will look for other ways to satisfy it – sensual satisfaction being one of them.

For reading & meditation – Mark 12:28-34

Sublimated desires

Do you not know that your body is a temple of the Holy Spirit, who is in you ...?
1 Corinthians 6:19

The sex drive is the creative urge, and physical creation is not the only way in which it can be fulfilled. Blocked on one level it can express itself on another. It can find expression in ways such as the creation of new systems of thought and new methods of helping and ministering to others. Some of the greatest work in the world has been done by those who, denied voluntarily or otherwise the normal outlets for the sex drive, turned this strange tide of power into other forms of creativity.

For reading & meditation – 1 Corinthians 6:12-20

Memories of the past

Forget the former things; do not dwell on the past.
Isaiah 43:18

Shame picks on those who have committed some grievous sin in the past – a sin which has been brought to the cross and forgiven – and works to make sure they will not forget it. Whenever they feel they have left the failure of the past far behind, his voice booms across the valley of their soul reminding them that even though God has forgotten their sin he will make sure they never forget it. Those tormented by him are filled with feelings of self-contempt that hinder them from moving on in the work of God.

For reading & meditation – Isaiah 43:14-28

Just holding the coats

Meanwhile, the witnesses laid their clothes at the feet of a young man named Saul.
Acts 7:58

Stephen prayed in his last moments: "Lord, do not hold this sin against them" (v. 60). Paul was there. No wound on the martyr's body could be attributed to him. He had simply been looking after the coats of those who murdered him. But in the language of today, he was an accessory before and after the fact. Though he might have said to himself, "I had nothing to do with it," the blood of the first martyr was on his hands. Yet Paul found forgiveness. And years later, he said: "Forgetting what is behind and straining towards what is ahead, I press on towards the goal ..." (Phil. 3:13-14).

For reading & meditation – Acts 7:54-60

What it means to "forget"

... he is short-sighted and blind, and has forgotten that he has been cleansed from his past sins.
2 Peter 1:9

Some psychologists tell us that it is impossible to forget anything. All our thoughts (they claim) are stored up inside us, and though they may be beyond the reach of recollection they are not outside our mental make-up. We may not be able to recall them at will, but they are not forgotten. Sometimes, of course, an accident or a trauma will produce what is known as amnesia (loss of memory). Give God the chance and he will make you forget anything that would be harmful to remember. Not the event, but the acute recollection of it.

For reading & meditation – 2 Peter 1:1-11

NOVEMBER 26

Repenting of "repentance"

Godly sorrow brings repentance that leads to salvation and leaves no regret ...
2 Corinthians 7:10

The path to God is the path of repentance. Yet so often our repentance is not what it should be. Often our repentance is not really repentance at all. It is only remorse or fear. We can be sad, even in tears, not because of the wrong we have done but because we have been found out or may yet be found out. Many have no sense of forgiveness because they have not really repented. Remember, repentance is not only being sorry for sin but being sorry for the self-centredness that prompted the sin in the first place. Sin is self in the place God ought to be.

For reading & meditation – 2 Corinthians 7:1-16

Remembering to forget

For I will forgive their wickedness
and will remember their sins no more.
Jeremiah 31:34

Haven't we been cast down not by genuine sorrow over sin but because we have suffered some personal deprivation? What does God say to a truly repentant people? "I will ... remember their sins no more." Note the phrase "I will remember no more." Whether or not God can forget is a moot point. The reality is that he remembers to forget. This might seem to be playing with words but the truth we all ought to exult in today is this: when we repent of our sin – truly repent – then the forgiveness that God gives is absolute and eternal.

For reading & meditation – Jeremiah 31:31-37

Righting wrongs

... if I have cheated anybody out of anything,
I will pay back four times the amount.
Luke 19:8

Though restitution may not be mentioned in modern-day sermons it is certainly mentioned in the Bible. Restitution is the attempt to make reparation for the damage we may have caused by our sin. Of course restitution isn't always possible, but it is something that we should always aim for nevertheless. And we must be clear also that it isn't restitution that wipes out the sin; it is the forgiving grace of Christ.

For reading & meditation – Luke 19:1-9

On forgiving yourself

Who will bring any charge against those whom God has chosen? It is God who justifies.
Romans 8:33

If you have genuinely repented, God has eternally and absolutely forgiven you. God has forgiven me; have I forgiven myself? When a sense of shame remains after having been forgiven by God, one ought to suspect the presence of pride. What you may be saying to yourself at some deep level of your emotional life is this: "How could I have ever done that? Me, of all people?" Hear the pride? Self-hate and self-contempt is rooted in pride, so recognise what is going on and repent even of that. Now, just as you forgive others, forgive yourself. God has forgiven you.

For reading & meditation – Romans 8:28-39

DECEMBER

Under the broom tree

[Elijah] came to a broom tree, sat down under it and prayed that he might die.
1 Kings 19:4

Elijah knew what it was to have an encounter with the giant of despair. Jezebel predicts that Elijah's life will be over within twenty-four hours. Finally he sinks in utter despair beneath the broom tree and says: "I've had enough, Lord. Take my life". God ministered to him by allowing him to take a long rest and providing a meal or two. Later he gave him a close friend by the name of Elisha to encourage him. Gently he prodded the prophet to get a new perspective on things. Elijah came back from despair. And so can you.

For reading & meditation – 1 Kings 19:1-21

Spiritual highs and lows

We were under great pressure ...
so that we despaired even of life.
2 Corinthians 1:8

The apostle Paul appears to have become despondent during his great missionary journey into Asia. Paul's despair and Elijah's despair took quite different forms. The prophet's despair was of such a nature that he wanted his life to end. The apostle's despair was because his life might end. But they were both affected by despair nevertheless. Why did God allow such a thing to happen to the great apostle? This is how Paul understood it: "that we might not rely on ourselves but on God" (v. 9). God can use even despair to advance his purposes for us.

For reading & meditation – 2 Corinthians 1:1-11

It can be done

The Lord gave and the Lord has taken away; may the name of the Lord be praised.
Job 1:21

Job was a man who experienced both the loss of those he loved and the things he loved. One after another the calamities struck. Job lost those he loved – his ten sons and daughters – and the things he loved – the herds which made him wealthy. How did he respond? He was devastated but not in despair. He didn't blame God and he didn't sin. He worshipped. Imagine that! It's difficult not to fall victim to the giant of despair in such circumstances, but as Job shows, it can be done.

For reading & meditation – Job 1:1-22

Three cardinal virtues

And now these three remain: faith, hope and love.
1 Corinthians 13:13

As we probe deeper into the dynamics of despair we find that the greatest loss is the loss of hope. The dictionary defines despair as "a complete loss or absence of hope; thing that causes this whether by badness or unapproachable excellence". Many think of hope as being precarious, an illusion, a vanity, a dream. "Hope is the most hopeless thing of all," said one cynic. How different is Scripture's view of hope. Paul tells us in today's passage that it is one of the three cardinal virtues of the Christian faith. But for hope to be real hope it must be linked to Christ. All other hopes are illusions. Only in Christ can hope be spelled with a capital "H".

For reading & meditation – 1 Corinthians 13:1-13

Tied to God's ends

Yet this I call to mind and therefore I have hope.
Lamentations 3:21

The world's view of hope is quite different from that of Scripture. Paul speaks of the patience or endurance of hope (1 Thess. 1:3), and hope that does not disappoint us (Rom. 5:5). The author of the epistle to the Hebrews makes what seems a paradoxical statement when he likens hope to an anchor for the soul that is firm and secure (Heb. 6:19). There is genuine hope and there is counterfeit hope. Optimism alone is not enough to save us from despair. We must have Christian hope: hope that is tied to good ends – God's ends.

For reading & meditation – Lamentations 3:19-33

DECEMBER 5

"The larger story"

... the God we serve is able to save us ... But even if he does not ...
Daniel 3:17-18

The Christian moves into life not inflated with foolish optimism but with a quiet and unquenchable hope drawn from the depths of our faith. And the language which comes easily to optimists is avoided by us. Confident boasting of a victory or wishful anticipation that things will go the way we think they should is not what Christian living is all about. It is based not on what we think is best but what God thinks is best. So perverse is our human nature that we prefer not only to write our own story but to direct it, produce it and star in it also. Often things don't go our way because they are going his way.

For reading & meditation – Daniel 3:1-30

Beating a hasty retreat

We are hard pressed on every side, but not crushed; perplexed, but not in despair ...
2 Corinthians 4:8

Despite all appearances to the contrary God is at work and he is good. When life falls to pieces all around you it is not easy to believe that God is active. And it is certainly difficult to believe that God is good. The cross gives the lie to that. Though circumstances may appear desperate, in reality that can never be so. Take your stand at the cross and hold on to that. Hope, remember, is more than optimism. When the shallow hopes of the world are dead, hope on in God. Then, like the apostle Paul, you will be able to say: "We are perplexed, but not in despair."

For reading & meditation – 2 Corinthians 4:1-18

DECEMBER 7

The tallest Titan

Pride goes before destruction, a haughty spirit before a fall.
Proverbs 16:18

In the Bible pride is portrayed as the primal sin. This is what turned an angel into a devil and, in turn, emptied heaven of a host of angels (Jude v. 6). But how can pride be defined? Pride is the ego in the place God wants to be. This is the essence of this awful soul disease. It puts self in the centre. It struts and shouts and brags. It has the attitude "I ... I ... I." It dethrones the Almighty in the human heart and instates the puffed-up ego. It gives self, not God, the supreme position. Such is its ruinous nature that William Law said of it: "Pride must die in you or Christ will not be able to live in you."

For reading & meditation – Proverbs 16:9-20

The devil's handiwork

When I consider your heavens ... what is man that you are mindful of him ...?
Psalm 8:3-4

When men and women claim to be the measure of all things, to be able to run their own world (how did it become theirs?), to solve their own problems, secure their own salvation, and manage their own destinies, they push God aside and take over his role in the universe. Indeed, as one person has put it: "The principle of pride, when taken to its nth degree, is capable, in intention at least, of pushing God out of the very universe he made." Pride is not a half-harmless sin. It is the devil's finished handiwork.

For reading & meditation – Psalm 8:1-9

Shallow thinking

When pride comes, then comes disgrace,
but with humility comes wisdom.
Proverbs 11:2

Pride not only denies that God is the Creator and Upholder of the universe, but relegates every other person to a minor role in it. The really proud man or woman never sees other persons as equal but as inferior, as minor actors in a play in which he or she is the leading character. When we really understand what pride is we realise it is the greatest sin of all. One commentator says of it: "It can even make virtues vicious and the other vices more vicious than they were." It is shallow thinking that dismisses pride as half-harmless, a thing to be brushed aside with a tolerant smile.

For reading & meditation – Proverbs 11:1-11

One great snare left

For everyone who exalts himself will be humbled,
and he who humbles himself will be exalted.
Luke 18:14

The Pharisee stood in the Temple, looked up to heaven and said: "God, I thank you that I am not like other men – robbers, evildoers, adulterers – or even like this tax collector. I fast twice a week and give a tenth of all I get" (vv. 11-12). And it was all true. He was not lying. He did not trace his advance in his spiritual life to the grace of God. He thought he had achieved it. The tax collector was different. He cried out, "God, have mercy on me, a sinner" (v. 13), and went back to his home justified. One individual had God at the centre of his life; the other had ... himself.

For reading & meditation – Luke 18:9-14

One hell ... one heaven

The proud and arrogant man – "Mocker" is his name; he behaves with overweening pride.
Proverbs 21:24

Nothing is more hateful to God than self-righteousness because it treats the blood of Christ as worthless and thus regards Calvary as unnecessary. But how do we combat pride? We can do so by resorting to the stone of truth and aiming it at the giant with the assurance that the battle is God's. And the truth that seems to have most helped people overcome pride is the truth about Christ, as recorded in the four Gospels. In Christ's light evidences of pride that are hidden in the dark crevices of the soul are revealed and seen as abhorrent.

For reading & meditation – Proverbs 21:20-31

The marks of pride

Who, being in very nature God ...
made himself nothing ...
Philippians 2:6-7

Is status all important to you? Is that what you are proud of? He who was God of very God laid it all aside and confined himself to a virgin's womb. Are you proud of your birth and your family? He grew up in a poor home in Nazareth. Are you proud of your profession? He was a carpenter. Are you proud of the social circle in which you move? He moved mainly among tax collectors and sinners. Are you proud of your abilities? He said: "By myself I can do nothing" (John 5:30). Are you proud of your position? He said: "I am among you as one who serves" (Luke 22:27).

For reading & meditation – Philippians 2:1-11

What an amazing sight!

I have set you an example that you should do as I have done for you.
John 13:15

During the meal Jesus gets up from the table and proceeds to wash the disciples' feet. It was his answer to their pride. It was an act done deliberately to emphasise the point that greatness lies not in being served but in serving. In dramatic terms it sets forth the need for selfless service which would later be exemplified by our Lord's death upon the cross. One Gospel tells of the disciples arguing among themselves during this meal (Luke 22:24-27), and by washing their feet our Lord in one stroke sweeps from their minds the idea that the great are those who lord it over others and remain "uncontaminated" by menial tasks.

For reading & meditation – John 13:1-17

DECEMBER 14

The invasion of revenge

Do not seek revenge or bear a grudge against one of your people ...
Leviticus 19:18

There is a great dissimilarity between those knocks where no ill-will was intended and those caused because someone deliberately set out to hurt. Counsellors know that the most difficult wounds to heal are those inflicted intentionally. The stab that was meant to injure; the hurt that was cruelly and consciously planned. These are the wounds which fester, and in some people generate a passion for vengeance that can remain in their heart until the day they die. If you are having a battle with the giant of revenge then make up your mind that the battle must come to an end.

For reading & meditation – Leviticus 19:1-19

A germ in the mind

Do not take revenge, my friends,
but leave room for God's wrath ...
Romans 12:19

The passion for revenge is like an evil germ in the mind. It breeds bitterness, depression and disease. Sometimes it is a factor behind mental unbalance and nervous breakdowns. The longing to "get even" can do more harm to a person harbouring that desire than the one or ones who caused the desire for revenge in the first place. Bitterness and the desire for revenge may be a compensation to a mind overcome with sorrow but not to those with whom they live. To cultivate the germ of resentment in the mind is as harmful as cultivating a germ or virus in the body.

For reading & meditation – Romans 12:9-21

Sand in the machinery

See to it that ... no bitter root grows up to cause trouble and defile many.
Hebrews 12:15

If the desire for revenge is not dealt with, it will soon turn a vengeful person into a morose, sour, embittered individual. Our whole being – body, soul and spirit – will not function at its best when we harbour bitterness and resentment. We are not created for hate; we are created for love. When we hate we violate the design which God built into us. We are less than we were meant to be. When we say of another, "He burns me up," that's true. Though you want to burn him or her up all you succeed in doing is burning yourself up. The desire for revenge is sand in the machinery of living. It fouls it up.

For reading & meditation – Hebrews 12:14-29

DECEMBER 17

The havoc of hate

Get rid of all bitterness, rage and anger, brawling and slander, along with every form of malice.
Ephesians 4:31

"Love your enemies, do good to those who hate you, bless those who curse you, pray for those who ill-treat you" (Luke 6:27-28). Did our Master set an unattainable standard and make an impossible demand? There are some who claim normal people cannot be free of the desire for revenge. They are probably right so far as those who do not know the grace of God are concerned. But they are quite wrong when it comes to those who do. Throughout time Christ has entered the lives of men and women who have been consumed with hatred and has eradicated all their desire for revenge.

For reading & meditation – Ephesians 4:17-32

The spirit of the cross

Jesus said, "Father, forgive them, for they do not know what they are doing."
Luke 23:34

The first person ever to die for Christ was Stephen. He was unjustly murdered. But Christ lived in him and loved in him. The more territory Christ occupies in our heart, the more effective will be his influence on what we say or do. The spirit of forgiveness expressed in the first words Christ spoke from the cross – "Father, forgive them" – can be found in your heart if you allow Christ to have full sway in your life. In his strength you too can forgive injuries, pray for your enemies, and love them to the end.

For reading & meditation – Luke 23:43

The right thing to do

Forgive as the Lord forgave you.
Colossians 3:13

The ony way to slay the giant of revenge is by the smooth stone of forgiveness. But is forgiveness always effective? Jesus' prayer of forgiveness after the soldiers had hammered him to the cross – "Father, forgive them" – does not appear to have broken the stony hearts of these men. Was it then a useless prayer? No, for the attitude of forgiveness was the right attitude to exhibit. They could hammer the life out of him but they could not hammer the love out of him. It was the Godlike response to evil. Forgiveness, whether it is received or not, is always the right response.

For reading & meditation – Colossians 3:1-17

DECEMBER 20

Free!

When they hurled their insults
at him, he did not retaliate ...
1 Peter 2:23

C*hrist forgave them*. He cried to God not for vengeance but for forgiveness. He handed the responsibility for judgment over to his Father. Second, *he prayed for them*. There is nothing like prayer to scour hate out of the heart. *He served them*. Their wickedness and sin could not deter him from loving. He was as free to escape from the cross as he was to walk away from the cliff-top at Nazareth when the people wanted to hurl him off. Put your hand in the stream of God's provisions and you will find the stone you need to defeat the giant of revenge once and for all.

For reading & meditation – 1 Peter 2:13-25

The "poor me" syndrome

Pray that you will not fall into temptation.
Luke 22:40

Like all the giants we have looked at previously self-pity relies upon threats and intimidations to make his conquests. Self-pity is particularly successful with those who feel life has never given them a chance, those who have been hampered from the start by some difficult circumstances. Self-pity, acts as an anodyne (a pain-killer) to the soul. It is often called the "poor me" syndrome as it causes people to focus on themselves and their own feelings rather than facing the issues of life with courage. When our misfortunes dominate our thoughts then temptation has even greater power.

For reading & meditation – Luke 22:39-46

No bed of roses

Your enemy the devil prowls around like a roaring lion looking for someone to devour.
1 Peter 5:8

Self-pity is a solvent that dissolves faith and pushes a person deep into doubt, where they find constant reasons for thinking that God does not keep his promises and that he forgets, at times, to be gracious. Self-pity also makes one entirely self-centred so that one's own petty problems become of greater concern than the tragedies affecting the lives of others. The worst thing about self-pity is that it exposes a person to temptation. When faith ebbs it is easy to become careless. But remember, no matter how hard life is, self-pity is ot the answer. Though it may bring temporary ief it is not a permanent solution.

For reading & meditation – 1 Peter 5:1-1

"Be happy – it's Christmas"

Surely he took up our infirmities
and carried our sorrows ...
Isaiah 53:4

Many feel worse at Christmas-time than at any other time of the year. Statistics show that more people suffer from depression at Christmas, and suicide rates often rise during this period also. If dark thoughts fill your mind this Christmas-time remember that God in Jesus took upon himself the heaped-up sorrows of the whole human race and, however unfriendly the world may seem to you today, Jesus knows and cares. All he asks is that you acknowledge your need of him and he will be there to help you and sustain you. Just kneel in prayer before him now and ask for his help.

For reading & meditation – Isaiah 53:1-12

Some unfamiliar aspects

... Mary ... was pledged to be married to him and was expecting a child.
Luke 2:5

Jesus' family tree was nothing to boast about. David is there, but so is Bathsheba. Ruth is there, but so is Rahab the harlot. Does your ancestry give you concern? Then no one understands you better than Jesus. Perhaps you feel you have always been at a disadvantage because you lost a parent early in life. There is a tradition in the Church that Joseph died while Jesus was still young. The years in Nazareth would not have been easy for him. He busied himself at the bench as a carpenter and was thirty before his ministry began. In the presence of One who had so much against him dare you say "I never had a chance?"

For reading & meditation – Luke 2:1-20

Truly worth remembering

... for Christ's sake, I delight in weaknesses, in insults, in hardships, in persecutions, in difficulties.
2 Corinthians 12:10

The apostle Paul was able to make it through life without feeling sorry for himself. Perhaps you are now saying : "But Paul was an exceptional man. I am just an ordinary person with no great advantages." Then listen to the testimony of Dr Robert C. Barnes, professor of counselling at Hardin-Simmons University in the USA. When he was thirteen he was struck down with polio – just two years before the polio vaccine became available. He said: "I knew that no disease, no accident, could take anything away from me that I needed in order to fulfil the purposes the Creator had for my life."

For reading & meditation – 2 Corinthians 12:1-10

Wanted at a wedding

... and Jesus and his disciples had also been invited to the wedding.
John 2:2

We do not know at what point the awareness came to Jesus that he was the Son of God and had a mission to save the world, but it is clear that once he was aware of it he knew what it would entail. The temptation to indulge in self-pity would have been enormous. But he moved forward resolutely, doggedly, courageously. His courage came from knowledge of the fact that nothing could happen to him without God permitting it, and that everything God permitted he would use. Hold on to that and you too will be invincible.

For reading & meditation – John 2:1-11

A great teacher

I can do everything through
him who gives me strength.
Philippians 4:13

Do you feel you have a lot to complain about? No physical or psychological difficulty can prevent God using us – as long as we yield ourselves to him. Remember a day is coming when you will stand before God and be expected to give account. Will you plead a physical disability with Helen Keller standing at your side? Will you come up to the throne and whisper "illegitimate" with Alexander Whyte standing there? With God difficulties can be made to yield a spiritual profit. Adversity is one of our greatest teachers. And God uses it to polish his jewels.

For reading & meditation – Philippians 4:10-20

All is not lost ...

And God is able to make all grace abound to you ...
2 Corinthians 9:8

Don't be so foolish as to envy those who seemingly have every advantage in life; the absence of advantage is sometimes the greatest advantage of all. Let everything spur you on towards God and his grace. Go forward in hope. God is above you, Christ and the Holy Spirit are within you, the angels of God are around you – what more do you need? Life may not have given you much of a chance, but in God you have every chance. All is not lost while you have courage. And Christ excels in giving that.

For reading & meditation – 2 Corinthians 9:6-15

The sword of Goliath

David said, "There is none like it; give it to me."
1 Samuel 21:9

Ahimelech offers David consecrated bread. Having been given the bread David then asks Ahimelech if there is a sword he can have and is told that lying behind the ephod is the sword of Goliath. "There is none like it," says David, "give it to me." The sword that was once used against him in an attempt to secure his destruction is now about to be used by him in his own defence. That same truth can be put this way: in every obstacle there is an opportunity, in every difficulty a door, and in every stumbling-block a stepping-stone. In God's service everything can be used – everything: the good, the bad and the indifferent.

For reading & meditation – 1 Samuel 21:1-9

Never too late

... the Anakites were there ... but, the Lord helping me, I will drive them out ...
Joshua 14:12

Don't settle for the *status quo*. If there are giants threatening you that need to be slain, go and get 'em. First, don't run. Stand your ground. The Lord of hosts is with you. Second, don't dress up in Saul's armour. Natural defences and resources are not much help in times of spiritual battle. Third, dip your hand in the cool, clear stream of God's Word and pick up one of the smooth stones of truth. Fourth, put it in your sling to signify your willingness to do battle. Then fifth, with a strong confidence in the Lord take aim. One to be ready. Two to be steady. Three to be off. Shoot!

For reading & meditation – Joshua 14:6-15

DECEMBER 31